Beautiful
CACTI

Beautiful
CACTI

A BASIC GROWER'S GUIDE

Gerhard Gröner
& Erich Götz

 Sterling Publishing Co., Inc.   New York

Thelocactus bicolor
(color photo on
page 2)

Translated by Elisabeth E. Reinersmann
English translation edited by Keith L. Schiffman

Library of Congress Cataloging-in-Publication Data

Gröner, Gerhard.
   [Schöne Kakteen. English]
   Beautiful cacti : a basic grower's guide / Gerhard Gröner & Erich
Götz ; [translated by Elisabeth E. Reinersmann].
      p.   cm.
   Translation of: Schöne Kakteen.
   Includes index.
   ISBN 0-8069-8504-6
   1. Cactus.   I. Götz, Erich, Dozent Dr.   II. Title.
SB438.G7613   1992
635.9′3347—dc20   91–38790
                                           CIP

10 9 8 7 6 5 4 3 2 1

English translation © 1992 by Sterling Publishing Company
387 Park Avenue South, New York, N.Y. 10016
Original edition published under the title
Schöne Kakteen © 1990 by Eugen Ulmer GmbH & Co.,
Wollgrasweg 41, 7000 Stuttgart 70
Distributed in Canada by Sterling Publishing
c/o Canadian Manda Group, P.O. Box 920, Station U
Toronto, Ontario, Canada M8Z 5P9
Distributed in Great Britain and Europe by Cassell PLC
Villiers House, 41/47 Strand, London WC2N 5JE, England
Distributed in Australia by Capricorn Link Ltd.
P.O. Box 665, Lane Cove, NSW 2066
Printed in Hong Kong

Sterling ISBN 0-8069-8504-6

CONTENTS

PREFACE

The cactus, a houseplant that's almost problem-free, has steadily increased in popularity. Its ability to adapt to dry climates allows a cactus to get by with very little humidity, making it an ideal indoor plant for living spaces heated with dry, hot air. Most cacti will tolerate dry spells lasting up to two or three weeks without showing any sign of damage. The owner can go on vacation worry-free. We all know what a problem it can be to find a "plant sitter."

Due to the increasing popularity of cacti, many nurseries, flower shops, and specialty stores now carry an ever increasing variety of them, including some rare species that were seldom seen until now.

Many plant and flower enthusiasts, having purchased a few cacti and having discovered the joy of seeing them grow, would like to know more about their "guests" from faraway places. They're interested in learning more about other varieties and types. This work is meant not only for beginners, but for all those who'd like to add to their existing collections. In addition to information about the care of cacti, we've tried to point out to the reader the beauty, the great variety of shapes, and the many different spines and flowers.

Gerhard Gröner and Erich Götz

STRUCTURE AND BEHAVIOR OF CACTI

Like many other plants, cacti are considered succulents. Due to the thickness of their leaves and stems, these plants are able to store a large amount of water.

What Are Succulents?

It's easy to distinguish leaf-succulents, like aloe, agave and other thick-leaved plants, from "leafless" stem-succulents. Some of the leaf-succulents (at first glance) look much like stem-succulents, like those of the Spurge (Euphorbia), and Stapelieae groups. However, observed in bloom it's clear that these leaf-succulents are not closely related to cacti. Even when not in bloom, it's easy to distinguish between cacti and members of the Spurge and Stapelieae groups. With the latter, little drops of a white, milky substance will appear after only the slightest injury. Only a few barrel cacti have this characteristic.

Succulents regulate their need for water in a way that's fundamentally different from other plants. While an ordinary plant with insufficient water supply will begin to wilt or dry out after a few days (or at the latest after a few weeks), succulents, with their ability to store water, can withstand weeks of total

Echinocactus grusonii. "Golden barrel" cactus. In a botanical garden this cactus can grow up to 3⅓ feet (1 m) in diameter.

drought without sustaining any damage. In addition, water evaporation is very slow due to the succulents' relatively small surface area.

Very few plants are as robust and demand as little care as succulents. It's no wonder that they're among the favorite indoor plants. It still pays to know something about their way of life, their structure, and their place of origin. This knowledge should greatly simplify the care they *do* need.

Cacti—Adaptation to Arid Climates

SHAPE OF CACTI

The rather curious appearance of cacti can be almost exclusively explained as an adaptation to arid climates. Without water, of course, even a cactus cannot survive.

Succulents handle the water that is available to them differently from non-succulent plants. A common green plant is 75% water, and sometimes even more. A small water loss that cannot be replenished through the root system causes the surface of the plant to close down its porous outer layer by closing the microscopic pores on the surface; this cuts water loss through evaporation by 10%. As this takes place, the plant is unable to absorb CO_2 from the air. CO_2 is essential to processing new organic substances. The plant will survive, but it will be unable to grow. A green plant can only afford to lose 50% of its water content. If it loses more than that, the plant will begin to wilt, and its leaves will dry up and fall off; the stem will also dry up very soon after.

Succulents operate on an entirely different system. Succulents are 95% water. If the roots are unable to absorb

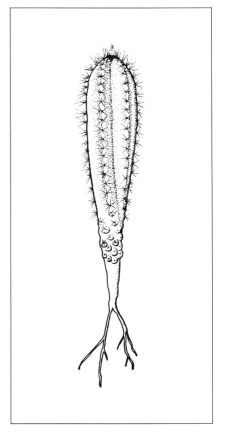

water, enough remains in their special water-storing tissue to sustain the green plant tissue for a considerable time. While water evaporates from the surface over a period of weeks, water lost is pumped back to the green tissue from the special water "reservoir."

Succulents have developed a special process for extracting CO_2 from the air with little use of water. During the day, pores on the surface remain closed. At night, however, when temperatures fall and relative humidity is higher (colder air is unable to hold as much humidity as warmer air) the plant opens its pores and evaporation is considerably less than it would be during the day. The CO_2 taken up, however, can only be converted into glucose and carbohydrates in the presence of light. The plant stores CO_2 temporarily in the form of malic acid (cell fluid is much more acidic during the night) to be used during the day for photosynthesis, which takes place while the pores on the surface of the plant are closed.

Succulent plants can quickly replenish water in their water-storing tissue. A cactus removed from the soil during a dry period shows small roots (the only means by which a cactus can absorb water from the soil) that are dried up and dead. If water is added to the soil, the cactus develops a rich amount of new small roots in just a few days, allowing the body of the plant to absorb water at a rapid rate.

The peculiar shapes of cacti are closely related to their way of life. The easiest way to create water-storing tissue is vividly demonstrated by the stem-succulents: They simply produce more or less swollen, fleshy shoots, or pads. Examples of such thick, column-shaped shoots can be observed on many of the genus *Opuntia*. These pads will simply fold into irregular shapes when water becomes scarce. Most *Opuntia*, however, have flat branches. Such

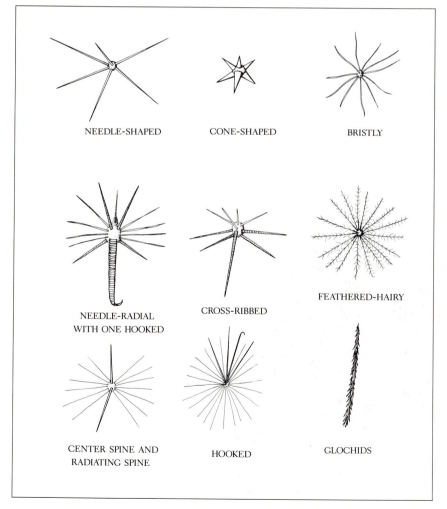

Types of cactus spines

NEEDLE-SHAPED CONE-SHAPED BRISTLY

NEEDLE-RADIAL WITH ONE HOOKED CROSS-RIBBED FEATHERED-HAIRY

CENTER SPINE AND RADIATING SPINE HOOKED GLOCHIDS

Left: Surface formation of an *Epithelantha*, grafted onto a *Trichocereus pachanoi*
Right: Branch of an *Opuntia microdasys*
Below: *Astrophytum myriostigma*, a very rare four-ribbed variety, with seeds

sectioning-off is *not* an example of growing leaves. From these new branches others can continue to grow, something leaves are unable to do. For a brief period, very young branches show small, narrow structures that can only be considered to be leaves.

When confronted with loss of water, some cacti (such as *Mammillaria* and *Rebutia*) do not change the shape of their surface very drastically. While they slowly decrease in size, spines will not lose their original, upright position.

Column-shaped cacti, which typically have a ribbed structure, are able to decrease their volume by folding like an accordion. However, very young column cacti will show this ribbed structure only after they have matured somewhat and early, elevated, spirally arranged spine-bundles begin to change and arrange themselves into vertical rows. (See the drawing on page 8.)

These spine bundles (or "areoles") identify a cactus. Branching or flowering takes place only from these points. Every areole has the capacity for growth, something that can be easily observed when cutting a column cactus. One or more of the areoles closest to the cutting surface will develop new growth. Areoles are very similar to "sleeping" buds from which spines, "wool," or bristle emerge. Some members of the genus *Opuntia*, however, grow frail leaves from the areole; in the case of *Pereskia*, even true, normal leaves can be seen. Areoles are shoots that have remained very short; in the case of cacti the botanist refers to these small spots as *glochidia*. The spines of the cactus represent "undeveloped"

12

leaves. Botanically speaking, they are "leaf-spines."

Cacti spines can appear in different numbers and differ widely in form and color. (See the drawing on page 9). Some species, like those of the genus *Mammillaria*, show spines that have developed into distinct center spines and radial spines. Spines on cacti serve as a very effective defense against grazing animals. The most effective spines are not the obvious, thick ones but rather the very small, short glochids of the *Opuntia*—they penetrate deep into the skin. Some of the hook-shaped spines, however, seem to serve another purpose. They attach themselves to the fur of an animal, which carries the spines over a great distance, assuring the spread of a particular species over a wide area. A very thick, light "mantle" of spines, on the other hand, serves to reflect most of the sun's rays, preventing the cactus from overheating. Studies have also shown that spines catch some of the morning dew and make it available to the plant. Defense against small insects is not the purpose of spines. Most cacti have a considerable amount of acid and crystals of calcium oxalate or a very slimy, bitter juice in their surface tissue that all serve to repel insects.

Aside from defending themselves against extended drought—and hungry animals—cacti have another problem to contend with: the drastic change in temperatures in the desert, where there is little other vegetation. It isn't unusual for the nighttime temperature to drop by as much as 68 °F (20 °C), sometimes even more. Here, too, the ability of cacti to store a great amount of water is very helpful. Since water is able to absorb and hold heat well, the cactus will not cool down as rapidly as the air surrounding it. Even moderate frost will

Eulychnia saint-pieana, **decorative even when still young, with its spines and hair, will seldom bloom.**

not harm cacti. However, most cacti have a very definite limit. Very few cacti can withstand a severe frost lasting more than a few days. Many cacti living in warmer climates will quickly sustain considerable damage when exposed to temperatures only slightly above freezing.

Damage from insufficient light will not be as evident as damage from frost. Over time, this lack of light will make it difficult or impossible for a cactus to survive. Cacti with very compact shapes can only absorb a relatively small

Gymnocalycium andreae

amount of light, and one might suppose that they will only survive in bright sunlight, but cacti are not very demanding, and they're able to manage (for a time) with little light. As long as they have enough water, cacti will survive. Like most plants, cacti will react to insufficient light with "stretching." Weak, watery tissue will reach towards light. A cactus will react to too much fertilization and to too much watering in a similar way. A cactus located in a shady place (and overwatered) might look particularly healthy. In reality, however, it's hungry, and it changes its shape by shifting the water inside without being able to build significant supportive tissue. Given a place with good light, a cactus will recover rather well, but it won't be able to correct the abnormal growth.

It's amazing to observe how many cacti do not need full sunlight, or even suffer from too much sunlight. Cacti, compared to other plants, grow very slowly.

Flower of an *Opuntia*

FLOWERING AND PROPAGATION

Flowers give cacti their special appeal. In contrast to their robust shape, cactus flowers are very delicate and short-lived, since they need only a few days of sunshine to attract insects for pollination. Like everything else in the life of a cactus, flowers take a long time to develop, sometimes several weeks. When they're ready, the buds burst open with lightning speed and often all on the same day. Pollination might be difficult because the flowers last for such a short time. In the case of a single plant, it seems reasonable that its internal "clock" will bring buds into flower all at the same time. However, since many different plants in a region come into bloom all at the same time, it's important that external stimulation is supplied, so that all plants are equally attractive to the insects. Temperature and the availability of water, as well as the amount of light, can differ over rather short distances. But the length of day

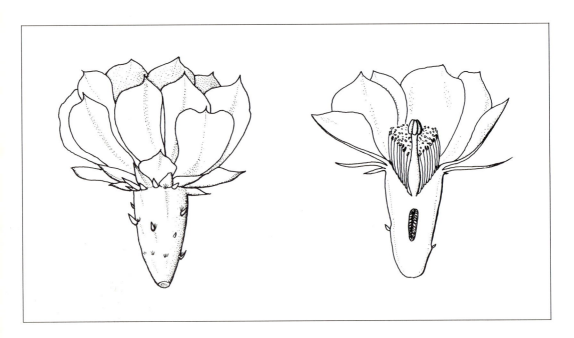

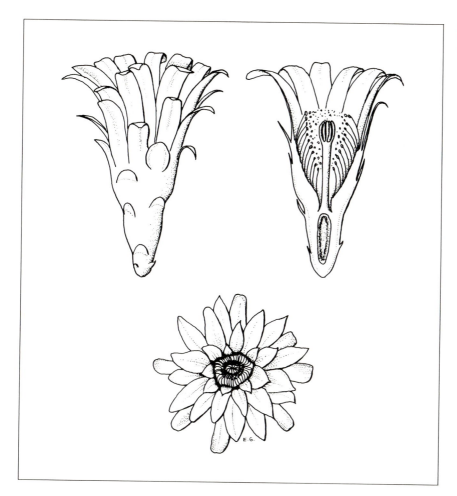

remains the same even over a wide area, and changes only with the change of the seasons. Obviously this is the precise signal for a plant to come into bloom. We know that a plant with a particular red pigment is able to register the length of daylight very accurately.

Cactus flowers present themselves in a very showy manner. (See the drawings on pages 14–18.) Small, short, tubelike, often lilac-colored flowers (like those of many *Mammillaria*), very effectively attract bees. Narrow, tubelike, bright red flowers, like those of the *Cleisto-cacti*, are typical bird-attracting flowers. Extremely long, tubelike white flowers

that open up at dusk and have a strong scent, with a good amount of nectar, are particularly attractive to moths. Some of the *Echinopsis* family have such flowers. Due to the number of stamens present in all cactus flowers, sufficient pollination is guaranteed. The nectar is found in deep, almost totally closed chambers at the base of the flower.

After pollination, seeds develop in abundance in either dried fruit or fleshy berries. Seeds need sufficient moisture to germinate. Seeds of almost all cacti are succulent from the beginning and need considerable time to grow. While cacti generally produce a great number

15

of seeds, germination in desert conditions is not very favorable. Often in the course of many years seeds are unable to germinate at all; and often those that do will perish during the early sensitive stage. Cactus seeds remain alive over a span of several years. With favorable conditions, many seeds will germinate. The year following germination is also very important for their survival. The ability of a young succulent plant to store water is relatively quickly exhausted. Because of the rather uncertain process of propagation by seed, asexual reproduction plays an important role for succulents and for cacti.

Many of the smaller species branch out into many smaller cacti, as is the case of *Mammillaria*. Other cacti of the genera *Echinopsis* and *Mammillaria* develop branches that are easily broken off. Any portion of a cactus that has been removed randomly will usually develop roots, like branches of an *Opuntia* or pieces of column cacti. *Opuntia* that have been severely damaged by animals have a good chance for survival. Even a small piece of a cactus containing an areole can generate roots and will then continue to grow. Many a cactus lover who wanted to propagate a rare species has made use of this knowledge.

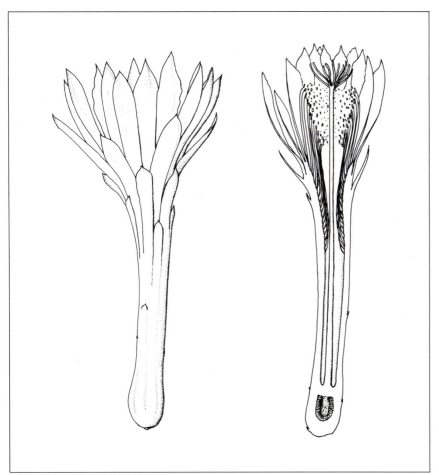

All cacti are very closely related, so it's possible to create a wide variety of hybrids from cacti that look rather different. This happens less often in nature, since individual species usually don't occupy the same area. Different cacti are found in different valleys, or the time of flowering differs by more than just a few days. Many members of the same cactus family often look remarkably different. Sometimes members of the same species living in the same place have different-colored flowers, as is the case among cacti of the genus *Lobivia*. Other differences (like the number and length of spines that are characteristic of particular cacti) are not as easily explained. They might be the result of genetic deviation or environmental conditions.

In principle, every cactus can be grafted onto any other cactus base; they will securely attach to each other. This is usually not nature's way. For instance, a shoot from an apple tree cannot be grafted onto a pear tree! It isn't known if such grafting occurs in nature.

Place of Origin

The presence of cacti in the wild is

17

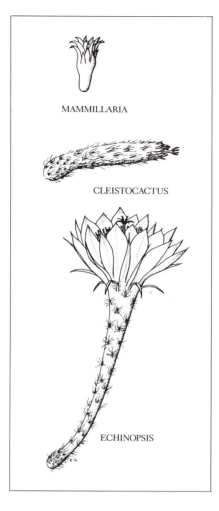

MAMMILLARIA

CLEISTOCACTUS

ECHINOPSIS

cacti, because almost no plant will grow on the desert floor. Only in restricted places, like valleys or mountain foothills, can one find plants, and then only a very limited number of species. Cacti are included, but only very few, and these are difficult to care for, so plant enthusiasts have shown little interest in them. The areas that are typically considered "cactus country" and are the home of the huge column cacti and *Opuntia*—Arizona, the Mexican highlands, southern California and some portions of the Andes in Peru—cannot be considered real deserts. Vegetation in these areas is usually very varied, and column cacti, which often reach the height of several yards (metres) and need many hundreds of quarts (litres) of water, are able to grow there in abundance. That succulents dominate the vegetation in an area does not imply that there's a shortage of water; it only means that water is available for a short time only and usually on an irregular basis. Huge cacti have adapted to that situation; their absolute need for water, however, is rather large. These large cacti, when transplanted to "civilization," need large amounts of water from time to time. It is more accurate to refer to the areas just mentioned as **cactus bush country** or **semidesert** rather than desert.

Smaller barrel cacti are also found in semidesert regions, but they're abundant in the **drier mountain areas.** Many of the *Mammillaria* come from the Mexican mountains, and those from the *Lobivia*, *Rebutia*, and *Sulcorebutia* genera are found in many parts of the Andes.

In the more **open and dry grasslands** of southern Brazil, Uruguay, and northern Argentina, many of the smaller barrel cacti, like the *Notocactus* and those

limited to the Americas. Those of the *Rhipsalis* family, found in the tropics of Africa, in Madagascar, and in India, are few in number and were most likely transported by sailing ships or birds. Even in the Americas, cacti are found primarily in areas with very dry climates. Two main regions constitute the home of the cacti: from Mexico to Arizona, and, in the dry climate of the Andes, stretching from Peru to Argentina and from there to the southern portion of Brazil.

The desert is generally not home to

of the *Gymnocalycia* and *Echinopsis* genera are found. They usually grow hidden in the protection of high grass; that's why they don't like direct, strong sunlight.

Other cacti make their home in entirely different environments, like those living in **tropical rain forests**. Here epiphytic cacti live in the branches of trees, like the Easter and Christmas cacti (which come from the coastal mountains of Rio de Janeiro) and those from the genus *Rhipsalis*. They're used to rather constant temperatures and humidity. It isn't surprising to find cacti in such an environment, since water runs off trees rather quickly, and the epiphytic plant is able to absorb and store it efficiently.

Cacti can be found in other very dry places where only a thin layer of sand or gravel covers rock formations.

It's not absolutely necessary for cacti to remain in conditions similar to their native environment. The epiphytic cactus, for instance, does not need a host plant and it grows just as well in soil. Plants growing in the mountains on rocks are not plentiful because they grow rather slowly and cannot compete successfully with more robust and faster-growing species. Cultivated and kept in a less stressful environment, however, they do quite well.

Examining the natural conditions under which cacti live makes it easy to determine what their needs are when you bring a cactus home. They are extremely undemanding; drought will not kill them. Too much moisture, however, causes rotting of the plant. Lack of sufficient light will eventually kill a cactus (very slowly), and it will cause unhealthy and unsightly growth. Depending upon their place of origin, different cacti will react differently to low temperatures. If the rhythm of the season they are used to is interfered with, they will continue to grow but (most of the time) they won't bloom.

PROPER LOCATION

There are several choices in your house or apartment where you can place plants and cacti. However, different cacti have different needs. The criteria discussed in this chapter will give the reader an idea of where to place a given cactus.

Places for Cacti in the House and Garden

WINDOW WITH MODERATE SUNLIGHT

Most cacti love light and sunshine. Most places in the middle of a room are not suitable. For Christmas cacti, for example, try a flower stand near a window not exposed to direct sunlight, but still with plenty of light.

Better conditions can be found at a windowsill that's not exposed to direct sunlight. Windows facing north or northeast, or a window that's shaded from direct sun by a tree or an adjacent building are all ideal. The light in such locations will come into the window from one side only. Try not to compensate for this one-sidedness by constantly rotating the plants. The temperature will be relatively cool during the summer months, but relatively warm during the winter months, provided the room is heated. Cacti from tropical forests do well in such places. Others like lots of light, but very little exposure to direct, hot sun and, in general, somewhat higher humidity. Christmas and Easter cacti belong to this last group.

Windows receiving sunlight for a few hours during the day (early in the morning or late in the afternoon) are ideal for some of the column cacti and ball cacti. Cacti suitable for this location have an overall green appearance. The dominant color of such cacti is green, and their bodies are covered by thick spines, a thick mantle of hair, or a frosty-white covering. The following cacti will do very well in such windows: *Mammillaria, Notocacti, Phyllocacti, Gymnocalycia, Cleistocacti,* and some members of the *Cereus* family, like the *Cereus peruvianus* (Peruvian apple cactus).

A window receiving sunlight for only a few hours during midday can cause problems. Only very robust cacti will be able to tolerate the stark differences in light and temperature created by the many hours of shade and the few hours of direct, hot sun. The gardener has to use his instincts when caring for plants in such a window.

SUNNY WINDOW

The windowsill that receives good sunlight and faces (generally) south or southwest is considered a difficult location. Light comes into the window from only one side. Temperatures will get hot behind the glass when direct sun reaches the window. If the sun hits a plant potted in a clay pot (and that pot is not inside another container), the soil will dry out rapidly on the exposed side and delicate roots might be burned.

Cacti (and some succulents) will do quite well in a sunny window, given proper care. Choose the "white" cacti, whose overall appearance is white due to dense, white (light-reflecting) spination or hairlike covering. Examples are "white" *Mammillaria, Astrophytia* that

are covered with white hair, some cacti from the genera *Echinocereus* and *Opuntia*, or from the genera *Thelocatus* and *Ferocactus*. The last two are not all white, but covered with a dense mantle of colorful spines.

BAY WINDOWS

A bay window with a sliding door to separate the flowers from the living room is an ideal place to grow cacti. Sliding doors allow the gardener to provide the ideal environment for plants. Pots can be set in a tray or a container filled with peat moss, preventing drastic changes in moisture and temperature. In addition, it's easy to increase humidity in an area that can be closed off, since the centrally heated air in the living quarters is usually rather dry.

If a window faces north or northeast (or if it's shaded by trees or a building and receives no sunlight at all) add variety to plants that prefer such a location (like tillandsia and orchids), and add Christmas and Easter cacti. Some hanging plants, like those of the *Rhipsalis* or *Aporophyllum* hybrid families, will do well in a bay window. White *Mammillaria* and *Astrophytia*, as well as *Ferocacti* and *Thelocacti*, thrive equally well in a sunny bay window, and a fascinating tropical environment can be created by adding some succulent *Euphorbia*.

LEDGE OUTSIDE A WINDOW

During warm weather, a ledge outside a window or a corresponding location on a balcony can be an ideal place for many robust cacti. Particularly during a wet summer, have some protection (like an overhang) against prolonged rain. Even the hardiest cacti don't like to be saturated. If rain should come occasionally from an unexpected direction, no damage is done. A quick shower washes off accumulated dust and the plant, refreshed and shiny, will thrive. Only excess rain causes damage. Cacti on a balcony or window ledge (rather than inside, on the windowsill) are afforded a more favorable range of temperatures and humidity. Since the sun is not filtered through glass, spines and flower buds will develop particularly well. Cacti from the genus *Echinopsis* and their hybrids grow splendidly in such a location, and they develop beautiful funnel-shaped flowers in great numbers. Cacti from the *Phyllocactus* family (in a wide variety of shapes), as well as the robust *Rebutia*, *Lobivia*, *Mammillaria* and *Notocacti*, also do very well in such a location.

SUMMER CAMP

Some cacti, particularly some of those from tropical forests, are able to spend the summer outside. They like fresh air and high humidity, and really don't want to be indoors during the summer months. For instance, the *Aporocati* (with long, tail-like growths) and the *Aporophyllum* hybrids could be placed in a partially shaded location, perhaps on a branch of a lilac bush. The same holds true for cacti from the *Rhipsalis* group, except that they prefer an even more shaded location. Other cacti, like the *Phyllocactus*, the "leaf" cacti (like the Christmas and Easter cacti) are also very fond of fresh air during the summer. Potted plants are usually too heavy to hang on branches. If they're placed on the ground they fall prey to snail attack. The solution is a flower stand positioned in the shade under a tree where the cacti can receive early morning and late-day sun. Other plants that do well in such places during the warm summer season are those of the genus *Selenicereus*, among them the famous "Queen of the Night," a night-blooming *Cereus*. Protect these plants from toppling over during strong winds by tying them securely to the stand. When rainfall is sparse, the whole plant can be easily watered with a watering can with a "sprinkler" head.

Barrel, ball, and column cacti can be placed outside if they're protected by a roof overhang from excess rain. Regular watering then becomes necessary. Be aware that a south-facing wall reflects

Cephalocereus senilis, "old man" cactus. This column-shaped cactus may grow several yards (metres) high in its native Mexico. The white hair makes it a favorite. Growers like to sell it when it's still very young.

the sun's heat. Some cacti thrive in such a location, like the large cacti from the genus *Echinocerus*, as well as large *Opuntia* varieties, or some of the column cacti. Pots for these cacti should be large enough to prevent rapid drying of the soil. The advice given for cacti placed on window ledges generally holds true for "summer camp" as well.

GARDEN HOTBED

Cacti connoisseurs once loved to get a head start by using a hotbed to grow their cacti. A wooden frame, a removable glass cover, and a layer of horse manure on the bottom were all that they needed. The use of this type of hotbed has largely been discontinued. What remains, however, is the desire to have a place for normal ball cacti and short-column cacti where they can enjoy an open-air environment in the summer without exposing them to the dangers of too much rain. The old type of frame has been replaced by a metal frame, placed on an asbestos-cement or concrete base. There's no contact with the ground. The sides and the cover are made from glass or Plexiglas. During warm weather, when it isn't raining, the lid is kept wide open; when it gets cool, and when it rains, the lid can be closed. This is important for the care of those cacti needing warm temperatures. The cacti are protected from excessive rain in this hotbed, and the temperature is also considerably warmer than it is outside. This is a definite advantage for cacti fond of warm temperatures. The gardener should be cautioned that if the lid has been closed due to rain, and later in the day the sun comes out, the temperature in a hotbed can get so high

Lobivia jajoiana. This flower with its black middle is considered one of the most beautiful among cactus flowers. The rim of the middle, outlined by a circle of stamens, can be clearly seen.

24

Lobivia jajoiana has several flowering varieties with different shapes and colors.

A group of "white" cacti

The yellow flowering cacti, *Astrophytum*. In front, *Mammillaria bombycina*; behind it, a type of *Mammillaria lanata*. Front right: a few *Mammillaria parkinsonii*.

(within half an hour) that severe burns to the surface of the cacti can occur, and the damage can last for years; sometimes cacti may not survive. It's better to leave the lid open just a crack (using a wedge or a pole). Greenhouses are sometimes equipped with automatic devices that open windows whenever the temperature inside reaches a certain point. These devices are also available for today's hotbeds, but they're seldom used.

Cultivation of cacti in hotbeds is seasonal because cacti should only be in a hotbed during their active growth phase. During the winter, cacti can be kept in an unheated room or in the basement, but they should be protected from subfreezing temperatures. Cultivation and care of cacti in a hotbed offer many possibilities for building a cacti collection. Robust cacti, particularly those native to higher elevations, used to more extreme conditions, do particularly well in a hotbed, often doing better than in a greenhouse. Almost all types and hybrids of the following genera—*Lobivia*, *Rebutia*, *Sulcorebutia*, *Trichocereus*, *Oreocereus*, *Echinopsis* (mostly those from the group of *Pseudolobivia*), robust *Mammillaria*, and *Notocacti*—will do well in a hotbed.

GREENHOUSE

The dream of many a cacti connoisseur is a greenhouse. Climate and growing conditions can be regulated, making it possible to grow those cacti that are very difficult to cultivate in a living room or in an open environment.

Appearance and What It Tells Us

We've looked at and discussed different locations in the house and in the garden where cacti can be successfully cared for.

The proper conditions for different cacti are referred to when their genus and their variety are discussed. What follows is a summary of those groups already discussed and the proper location for them.

Leaf cacti prefer high humidity but not too much sunlight. They're ideal for a bay window or for a windowsill facing north, northeast, or east. They thrive outdoors in the shade or half-shade under a tree or a bush during the summer. Members of this group include Christmas and Easter cacti, those from the genus *Rhipsalis*, and the *Phyllocacti*.

Cacti that are not protected by a large number of (or very strong) spines or hairs—the "**green cacti**"—like a well-lit and partially shaded location where temperatures are not too high. Ideal are windows facing east, southeast, or west. It's crucial that they be protected from direct, strong, midday sun. Many of these cacti can be cared for on an outside window ledge if the location is not exposed to heavy rainfall. **Green cacti** also do very well during the summer in a hotbed that isn't exposed to too much hot, direct sunlight.

The "**white cacti**," covered with thick and colorful (often radial) spines and a mantle of hair, like a south- or southwest-facing window or a bay window that receives direct sunlight. Since they like the higher temperatures found in such locations, and since they're usually sensitive to too much humidity, a stay on an outside window ledge, or in the garden during the summer months, is recommended only if adequate protection from rain can be assured. Also, a hotbed is a good place for this group of cacti during the warm season.

CARING FOR CACTI

In general, cultivating cacti isn't difficult. What's surprising is that we're able to care for so many cacti and that they grow and flower so beautifully, even in northern climates. After all, most come from climates totally different from our own. Theirs is a climate with sharply defined dry and wet seasons. In their native regions, the difference between summer and winter temperatures isn't as great as the difference between day and night temperatures.

Most cacti are robust, very adaptable and grateful plants. As soon as a gardener has mastered and implemented the basic points of cacti care, he'll be surprised to see how little work and time are necessary to make cacti grow and bloom.

Plant cultivation should always to be considered in its totality. Location, potting container, type of soil, and amount of care are all closely connected. For example, frequent watering is necessary for a plant that's on a very sunny, hot windowsill and that's planted in a small clay pot that allows water to evaporate easily.

Later in this chapter we'll discuss the following topics: soil, light, temperature, watering, and fertilizing.

Containers

The container is of great importance if a cactus is to thrive. It holds the soil and, therefore, the nutrients and moisture necessary for growth. Nurseries and flower shops offer cacti in rather small pots because they take up little space and they cost little. This is particularly true of those tiny clay pots that are used to sell miniature cacti. These small pots are not large enough for cultivating cacti because there isn't enough room for a plant to grow. A small pot will easily overheat when standing in direct sunlight and then it will cool down too rapidly after sundown. The soil dries out rapidly in the hot sun and the plant constantly lives between the unhealthy extremes of too wet (right after watering) and too dry, too hot and too cold. Since cacti are very robust, they won't show the result of such extreme conditions immediately. Cultivating a cactus in such a small container is very unsatisfactory. Nurseries wouldn't leave plants in such containers either, if they intended to sell them later as mature plants. Cacti in nurseries are often cultivated in large seed beds and only when they're ready for sale are they transplanted into small containers. Cacti are also transplanted into small clay pots and then set into larger containers (raised or on the ground) in the greenhouse, where optimal climate conditions can be created.

At home, however, the newly purchased cacti must be transferred from the small commercial container into a flowerpot large enough for further cultivation. How large a pot? There's no standard answer. A pot should be big enough to give the plant one or two years of continued growth and development, and small enough so that the root system has a chance to spread throughout the soil after an appropriate interval. Don't put a small plant into a huge pot. Because the root system can't grow through the soil thoroughly, the "empty" portion is an ideal place for conditions that foster rot. Small cacti are best planted several together in a large pot or in a dish.

CLAY OR PLASTIC?

The **clay pot**, the conventional container for all indoor plants, has advantages and disadvantages for cultivating cacti. A clay pot allows moisture to evaporate quickly; the rate depends on the location (sunny, hot, south window) and the degree of humidity in the air. The soil in a clay pot may dry out faster than the plant's need for water would indicate. The temperature in a clay pot can drop considerably due to rapid evaporation of moisture. Salts contained in the water used for watering the plants are deposited on the inside of the porous clay material. In regions with water having a particularly high lime content, these deposits create a very alkaline soil after a time. Almost all cacti prefer a slightly acidic soil. Alkaline soil causes roots to die, and the cacti will be lost. Clay does have its advantages. It remains rigid, which is an important advantage when compared to plastic, particularly when a plant calls for a large container. Clay pots are heavy and stand securely on any surface. This is an important consideration for tall and trailing plants. Sometimes rapid water evaporation is an advantage when a cactus has been watered too heavily and at the wrong time. Calcium deposits on the pot can easily be prevented by watering with softened water. The inside of clay pots can also be treated with a non-toxic sealer.

Clay pots come in many different shapes, and what can't be found in a flower shop can usually be found in nurseries. Use a wide, low container when several different cacti are to be arranged in one dish.

Plastic pots also have their advantages and disadvantages. The quality of the plastics used differs greatly. The gardener should not buy plastic pots used in a nursery; they're not meant to give a plant a permanent home. A pot made from rigid, stable plastic should be chosen instead. These pots are available in many different shapes, even low dish-like containers needed for cactus arrangements mentioned earlier. Only cacti with tuberous roots should be planted in a tall plastic pot. Plastic pots come in the usual round shape, and also in rectangular shapes, used particularly by nurseries.

Plastic flowerpots are inexpensive and easy to stack for storage. Thanks to their smooth surface they're easy to clean and they can be used over and over again. Since the material isn't porous, plants don't need to be watered as often as they would be in a clay pot. For inexperienced gardeners, this point can turn into a disadvantage. Plants in plastic pots need only about one third of the water used to water plants in clay pots. There is always a danger that plants in plastic containers may be watered too much and too often. Even if the top layer of the soil is already dry, the lower portion of the soil in a plastic pot is usually still moist. Cacti, however, do not need to be watered until all of the soil has dried out. As has already been mentioned, cacti do not like to stand continuously in wet soil. Furthermore, plastic pots deteriorate over time and they get brittle and crack easily. This is of particular importance for sun-loving cacti that are at the mercy of the heat created by direct exposure to the sun.

To summarize: Plastic containers are suitable for smaller cacti planted by themselves in one pot. It's difficult to regulate temperature and moisture

content in small clay pots; they overheat easily and evaporation is rapid. Plastic pots, without question, have a definite advantage.

Large cacti, however, require large pots. The larger volume of soil ensures a balanced condition of temperature and moisture. Also, larger plants need large, sturdy pots that keep their shape and remain stable. Where the danger of accidental breakage (for instance, when a pot is not lifted properly) doesn't exist, a clay pot has the advantage over plastic. If a plant has been overwatered accidentally, it can take a long time for the soil in a large plastic pot to dry out. Moist soil (over time) favors the growth of bacteria which can infect and damage the plant.

DISH GARDENS

Considering the disadvantages of cultivating cacti in small clay pots with the unstable conditions that may exist, one may want to plant several cacti together in a dish garden and thereby provide a larger and more balanced environment. Indeed, one can find (particularly indoors) beautiful arrangements with thriving cacti in dish gardens and flower boxes. The cactus connoisseur who has a greenhouse with the ideal environment may prefer to give each plant its own pot, unless he chooses to plant the larger cacti directly into a flower bed.

If you want to plant several cacti in a dish garden, first find a proper container. Flower shops usually have a good selection of round dishes, which are fine as long as they have a drainage device and the owner isn't tempted to place this dish in the middle of a table. Such a place would be too dark for cacti.

Bay windows that are constructed especially for growing plants are usually equipped with a large container already in place. For a windowsill, however, a regular flower box is more suitable. Some flower boxes are made specifically for indoor use and they look better than the outdoor type. Any flower box must have holes on the bottom to allow excess water to drain off. Outdoors, water drainage might not be a problem, but indoors a galvanized metal, or plastic tray must be used. Since it's often impossible to find the proper-size tray, buy a flower box already equipped with a tray.

Only healthy cacti of approximately equal size and with the need for similar environmental conditions should be combined. Avoid putting a fast-growing cactus next to a rare, slow-growing one, where the slower one would be crowded out. This "crowding" might happen in the soil, where the root system of a robust, fast-growing cactus takes over more and more of the space that the slow-growing cactus needs for survival. Also, one should not combine a "white" sun-loving cactus with a "green" cactus with less protective cover, since a green cactus needs protection from hot midday sun. Since cacti are planted in the same soil and soil-borne pests that attack the root system are able to spread unhindered, only the very healthiest of plants should be chosen.

The skilled indoor gardener can assure himself of beautiful results if he chooses the proper location of the box. Cultivating cacti in a box, however, might create a problem if a single cactus has to be removed (for taking a photo of one particular species, perhaps, or if a cactus has grown too large and must be planted in an individual container). The entire contents of the box may have to be replanted.

You can combine the advantages of individual pots and a dish garden by combining individual clay pots in a window box and filling the space between them with a mixture of peat moss and sand. The porous walls of the clay pots and the moisture in the peat moss mixture allow for a good moisture balance. Those cacti that need to be slightly moist in the winter can be accommodated by keeping the peat moss evenly but moderately damp. Cacti planted in plastic pots won't be able to take advantage of such an arrangement because such a moisture exchange cannot take place in plastic pots. Soil temperatures within a box filled with peat moss are even, whether clay or plastic pots are used. Dish gardens can be easily moved when necessary (when the window must be opened, for example).

Individual plants set in a box allow the gardener to easily remove one pot for repotting if a plant grows particularly fast. If a cactus is to be photographed, it can simply be taken out and put back again. The top edges of flowerpots in a dish garden can be easily hidden by placing small, decorative stones on top of the soil, creating an interesting landscape.

Soil and Substrate

Cacti thrive in many different substrates, as long as a few basic rules are observed. For instance, soil for cacti should be light and porous; it shouldn't become packed and silted up. Soil should not contain fresh compost, since it encourages rot. Soil should be slightly acidic (a pH of about 5.5). It should also be able to hold sufficient nutrients and moisture and it should be able to make it available to the plant slowly.

Cactus connoisseurs with an established large collection probably make their own soil mix and they'll have all the necessary ingredients on hand. Those with only a few cacti or a modest collection can buy prepackaged soil in a nursery. Commercial cactus soil is expensive, and it often doesn't contain all that's needed for cultivation. It might be better to buy regular potting soil. The structure of the potting soil should be stable, containing a certain amount of clay, and it should be free of damaging bacteria and weeds. Use such potting soil at a ratio of 1:1 with a porous material, like coarse sand or perlite. These ingredients increase the soil's ability to absorb moisture, and they allow the soil to breathe. A porous, stable, soil structure is important. Coarse sand is preferred over fine sand, or sand containing clay. For cacti that like humus soil, use a mixture of 60% potting soil and 40% filler (sand or perlite). For those cacti sensitive to excess moisture and that need only a small amount of water, the mixture should be reversed: 40% potting soil and 60% filler. Only for the very sensitive, rare cacti that come from an extreme climate is a special mixture necessary, usually one totally free of any humus. These species are generally cultivated only by the specialist.

Only the epiphytic cacti and those that live in the tropical forests are exceptions. Some of these are the Christmas and Easter cacti of the genus *Rhipsalis*, the *Selenicereus* (including the "Queen of the Night"), and many *Phyllocacti*. They prefer acidic humus soil that must be porous. Mix potting soil with ground sphagnum moss and some peat moss, as well as with perlite.

Light and Temperature

Plants need light and warmth; only then are their systems able to create (with the help of chlorophyll and photosynthesis) carbohydrates from the carbon dioxide in the air and in the water. The water is absorbed through the root system. Carbohydrates are necessary for a plant to grow and thrive.

Cacti come from regions of high elevation and little cloud cover where there is a great and intense amount of sunlight. Spines, hair, and a deeply ribbed surface covered with a waxlike substance, are all means by which cacti protect themselves from intense sunlight.

In order for cacti to thrive, they must have an environment that is as close as possible to what they are accustomed to. Most important is a proper amount of light. Lack of sufficient light will cause the cactus to lose its deep green color and to produce abnormal, rapid growth. Cacti that are by nature strong and stocky will become thin and weak, and they'll need support when deprived of sufficient light.

As was mentioned in the discussion about the proper location for cacti, all cacti need light, but the amount and intensity differ for different species. See page 31.

The majority of cacti want a lot of light and sunshine, but the change from dark winter days to increased spring light must take place gradually. This is of particular importance for cacti that have spent most of the winter in a dark place (a staircase or the cellar). The often very intense sunlight in spring may cause ugly burns on the surface tissue. It is best to choose a cloudy day when moving a cactus to its summer location and to provide some shade at the beginning, particularly on bright, hot days. If cacti are moved to a hotbed, a piece of light material can be put over the lid. It is also helpful to cover the window glass

of the hotbed with a thin layer of white paint; thin tissue paper spread out over the cacti is also very effective. The shade provided should only filter the sunlight, not eliminate it altogether. These precautionary measures can be discontinued as soon as the cacti have become accustomed to their new location.

Let's briefly look at what kind of light is appropriate for the cacti. In their native environment, under a clear sky, they enjoyed the full spectrum of sunlight. The light that reaches us in our cities is often diminished due to dust and pollution, and it's further diminished by window glass or hotbed covers. Ultraviolet light is almost totally filtered out by such glass. Whenever possible, give cacti unfiltered, full sunlight. This is particularly important at the end of the summer and in the autumn for the proper development of spines and new growth and for the development of flowers. Whenever possible, the window of the hotbed should be opened wide during summer and fall. Cacti spending the summer and fall on a rain-protected window ledge or on a balcony usually have particularly well-established, strong spines; they look healthy and produce a large number of flowers.

Most cacti rest during the winter when the growing phase has ended, although some bloom in the winter, like the Christmas cactus. Keep cacti during their resting period in a place with moderate light. The change back to their summer location will be only half as difficult, the danger of fungus infection will be much less likely, and the early-flowering cacti will develop much better buds. Some cacti do well spending the winter months in the dark, on a dark staircase or in the basement, as long as the place is dry and cool, so that the growth period truly stops. On mild days, fresh air may be supplied when possible.

If cacti are kept in a dark basement, artificial light can be used to give them the minimum amount of light that they require. Most cacti do not need artificial light (like fluorescent light), because they're in their rest period. Artificial light during the active growing season is absolutely useless. It is impossible to create the intense full-spectrum sunlight in a dark location no matter what type of light source is used. Tropical cacti, however, like those from the genus *Rhipsalis*, are different. Like orchids that come from a similar environment, it's possible to support the winter-flowering plant with artificial light during the dark winter months. If these cacti are grouped together with tillandsia and orchids in a bay window, they will thrive and bloom beautifully when nurtured by strategically placed artificial light.

Watering and Fertilizing

Watering cacti may be a problem for many gardeners. Some think that the cactus is a desert plant and needs very little water. Others water their cacti a little at a time but do so daily. Both methods are wrong. Once the basic needs of a cactus are understood, care is rather simple.

WHEN TO WATER

Normal cacti are watered only when they're actively growing, in bloom, or developing new branches or shoots. They should be watered during this period only when the soil has dried out. The more rapid the growth, the more water they need. In addition, when they're in a place where evaporation is rapid, the amount of water has to be increased. The reverse is also true. If they're in a cool location—the basement during the winter, for example—watering should be discontinued altogether. The metabolism of a cactus stops at temperatures of 50–70 °F (10–15 °C) The plant is unable to absorb water then, and moisture in the soil will lead to rotting.

Cacti shouldn't be watered at all during the winter months if they're moved to a cool location. Only cacti that remain in warmer locations like the window of a living room or tropical cacti should be watered, and then very sparingly. This means only a teaspoon or tablespoon of water every week. Cacti in clay pots set in large containers of peat moss are not watered directly; only the peat moss is kept moist. In the spring, when growth begins and flower buds

Aporocactus flagelliformis (rattail cactus). **An example of normal as well as cristate branches, the** *Aporocactus* **is a very popular hanging plant.**

begin to form, spray plants gently at first and water sparingly—without fertilizer! This spray washes away the winter dust and encourages the development of small suction roots. During the active growth period from spring until autumn, cacti are watered at intervals from one to three weeks. A definite rule is difficult to establish; the frequency depends upon location, temperature, the size and type of the plant, the soil, and the plant's growth rate. The basic rule is that a cactus is not to be watered until the soil is dry, and not only dry on the surface, but deep within the pot.

Some cacti—for instance, the *Rebutia*—need a rest period when they've finished blooming, During this time watering should be reduced. Miniature cacti with tuberlike roots and a dense, white spine cover (indicating that they come from a warm climate and are very efficient users of water) need less watering. Cacti with a deep green color and rapid growth, like the column cacti or genus *Echinopsis*, need to be watered more often. Starting in the fall, slowly reduce watering to give new growth time to mature and to allow the plant to prepare for the coming dormant period.

Exceptions to these watering instructions are the epiphytic and tropical plants. Here the soil should never dry out. These cacti should remain in a warm place even during the winter months. They usually bloom in the winter and, therefore, are in need of water all of the time. However, even epiphytic plants only want to be moist, and not saturated with water. Cacti should be watered during the warm, sunny portion of the day. If watered during the cool and damp portions of the day, they may remain in wet soil too long, which encourages rotting.

HOW TO WATER

Cacti shouldn't be watered every day, but rather at intervals of several days, and then watered thoroughly. One place where cacti are particularly susceptible to rot is at the base, the point where the body and the roots connect. Most cacti have a tuberlike root, with a small suction root further down in the soil, so watering from below is recommended. If a pot sits in a saucer of sufficient size, a generous amount of water can be poured into it. However, discard excess water that the cacti has not absorbed after a few hours. A cactus should never stand in a water-filled saucer for even one day. This watering method can also be applied to a dish garden, giving the cacti collection the optimal moisture it needs.

In principle, water should only be supplied to the soil, and not to the plant itself. Water could remain in crevices, and when exposed to direct, hot sun, might burn the surface tissue; during colder weather the development of fungus might be encouraged.

But you can give your cactus a good shower from time to time with clean water and without any fertilizer added. At the end of a hot day in the sun, this shower is very refreshing for cacti. The gardener who has cacti outside will notice how refreshed and healthy green cacti look after a thunderstorm. However, cacti that have a slightly blue tinge or a frostlike covering shouldn't get a "shower," since water might discolor their decorative covering. If the water contains too much lime, it may create unsightly splotches or the same discoloration.

Day and night temperatures often differ widely in the cacti's native environment. Such differences create dense fog or dew and high humidity at certain times of the day. Some cacti are able to absorb water through their surface tissue, spines, or hair. Many cacti become stunted when they live constantly in a very dry environment. Of course, this is the case in many living rooms, particularly when a cactus is placed in a warm, sunny south window. Such a place, with little humidity, is not good for otherwise problem-free cacti like *Rebutia*, *Lobivia* and *Echinopsis*.

FERTILIZING

Cacti come from regions that are usually rich in mineral salts, so it's wrong to think that cacti should not be fertilized. Fertilize at the right time, and with the proper fertilizer. In principle, cacti are only fertilized during their active growing season, between spring and late summer. At the beginning of the growth cycle, use only plain water without adding any fertilizer, and do the same at the end of the growing season in the fall, before the rest period begins.

Fertilizers differ in their chemical content. It's easy to distinguish between fertilizers that are high in nitrogen (to encourage growth) and those that are high in potassium and phosphorus (to encourage flowering). Cacti, in contrast to leaf-bearing, bushy plants, grow very slowly and need fertilizer with less nitrogen and more potassium and phosphorus. A combination of 4% nitrogen (N), 14% phosphorus (P), and 18% potassium (K) is recommended. Fertilizers should contain the trace elements magnesium, manganese, boron and others in order to ensure healthy growth, even if these minerals are present only in minute amounts.

Fertilizers with too much nitrogen result in unnatural, large growth. Such cacti are very susceptible to disease. Cacti should grow slowly, healthy and stocky. A fertilizer that's low in nitrogen and rich in potassium and phosphorus will give good results.

Of course, a gardener wouldn't think of mixing his own fertilizer unless he had a huge collection of cacti. Several good fertilizers specifically designed for the care of cacti are available. It's O.K. to use fertilizer especially mixed to encourage flowering. It's also O.K. to use guano now and then, even if it smells bad and doesn't dissolve entirely in water. Guano contains a rich combination of trace elements that are not always present in artificial fertilizer.

How much fertilizer is enough? Follow the manufacturer's instructions. Make sure that powdered fertilizer is completely dissolved before watering; otherwise some cacti get too much of one thing and others get too little of another. Mineral fertilizer should not exceed ¼ teaspoon (1 gram) per quart (litre) of water.

Repotting

Cacti should not be repotted on a fixed schedule (like once a year), but rather when it's necessary. It's time to repot when the pot no longer accommodates the plant, when the soil is used up, when one suspects an invasion of pests or fungi, or when growth and flowering seem to have stopped.

Newly acquired cacti should be repotted immediately. Nurseries usually put cacti in very small, space-saving containers that aren't sufficient for home cultivation.

The soil in the pot must dry out before you plan to repot. The best time to repot is either late winter or early spring. If it should become necessary to repot at any other time, make sure that the soil is completely dry.

Before you start, prepare a working space—a table in the backyard, a hobby room, or a kitchen table covered with newspaper. New, clean pots and relatively dry potting soil should be handy. A new pot should be big enough for a plant to be able to grow and develop, but it shouldn't be too big. When choosing a new pot, the gardener should also consider the type of root the particular cactus has. A cactus with tuberlike roots needs a deeper pot than one that grows several fleshy roots, for which a shallow pot is more suitable.

A gardener should avoid touching spines during repotting (it's in his own best interest). The plant shouldn't be pulled out of the old pot. Cacti will come out of their pots when they're in their rest period and the soil is dry, particularly when they've been planted in plastic pots. Loosen the top layer of the soil using a small wooden stick, and then discard the soil. The plant, including the root system, will usually slide out of the pot very easily. A plant in a clay pot, having a broken piece of pot over the drainage hole, is easily removed (after the surface soil has been discarded) by pushing gently from the bottom with a pencil or a wooden stick. This procedure pushes the plant out of the pot, roots and all. If a plant has become seriously pot-bound and won't budge, it might be necessary to break the pot—gently!

Using a wooden stick, very gently loosen the clumped-up roots. Used-up soil and old, dried-up roots are shaken off. This is the time to inspect the whole of the root system for possible pest or fungus infection. Particularly obvious is a root mealybug infection appearing as a chalky white deposit. If it's clear that most of the root system has rotted, cut back the roots to the healthy portion

using a sharp knife. The knife must be disinfected after each cut! The plant should be allowed to dry and then repotted like a cutting. (See page 50.) If the root system is healthy, the plant is ready to go into a new pot.

Cover the drainage hole with a small broken piece of pot and spread a layer of new potting soil over it. Set the plant in the middle of the pot at the same depth it was originally growing, and carefully fill in the soil around the plant. Use a tablespoon or a small toy shovel for this task. Knock the pot gently against the tabletop to allow soil to fill in all the spaces around the roots. When the pot is filled sufficiently, push the soil down slightly. However, don't pack down the soil. All cacti, particularly those with tuberous roots, are sensitive to moisture at the neck of the root. Therefore, use particularly porous soil in this area. Prepare such porous soil in advance in a separate container by adding a good portion of coarse sand to the potting soil. Use this mixture as the last top layer.

In contrast to other plants, cacti are not watered after repotting. Small injuries to sensitive roots usually can't be prevented during repotting. Injured roots are prone to rot when wet. For that reason, the repotted cacti are placed in a warm but shaded place for a few days and are watered only after these injuries have had a chance to heal. If large column cacti are not securely anchored in the soil immediately after repotting, they may tip over. Use a support pole to aid the cactus until a solid root system has been established.

The gardener may be injured by spines if a cactus is not handled carefully. Handle the plant as little as possible, and when it's handled do so very gently and without pressure. Work gloves or gardening gloves will provide some protection, but they're little help for the very thorny spines, and the spines of the *Opuntia*. These cacti should not be touched directly. Use a protective layer of old newspaper, a thick plastic bag, or two small wooden sticks (like chopsticks) to handle them.

If cactus spines have penetrated the skin, they should be removed using clean tweezers. A problem might arise when dealing with fine, hooked spines from the *Opuntia* cactus that can penetrate the skin, often in hundreds of places, by one inadvertent touch. Rubbing or washing the skin will only make the injury worse and will push those spines deeper. In such cases, light a candle and apply liquid wax to the injured skin. The wax will harden when held under cold water. Pulling off the hardened wax will take the embedded spines out with it.

How to Make a Cactus Bloom

Time and again, gardeners complain that although their cacti are thriving, they never bloom. Here are a few points about what makes a cactus bloom and what prevents it.

Even in their native habitat, some cacti will only begin to bloom when they're old and they've reached a considerable size. This is particularly true of column cacti. Many cactus seed mixtures contain a large number of column-cactus seeds because they germinate easily, the young plant grows rather quickly, and even a beginner will have the satisfaction of success. The indoor gardener should not expect that such cacti will bloom.

Some cacti will bloom after they reach a certain age, but much light and warmth are necessary for that to take

place. Many cuttings from wild cacti (particularly those from the genus *Opuntia*) have been brought home from Mediterranean vacations, and often these cuttings have grown into respectable cacti. Flowering, however, can only take place under very specific conditions. The same holds true for some cacti of the genus *Trichocereus*. Cuttings from the *Trichocereus schickendantzii* are endlessly passed from one cactus connoisseur to another. These cuttings grow into sizable groupings. However, flowering does not take place until the plant reaches a relatively large size, and then only with the finest fertilizer and very good growing conditions.

Cacti grown indoors also need to reach a certain age and size for flowering to occur, and the time needed differs markedly between genera and varieties. Some *Rebutia* bloom when they're two years old. Many *Mammillaria*, *Notocacti*, *Lobivia*, and *Gymnocalycia* will bloom in their third or fourth year. Some *Ferocacti* and *Trichocereus* won't bloom for ten to fifteen years.

Tuberous roots of
Sulcorebutia

37

As with all other plants, some cacti are eager to bloom and some are lazy bloomers. The latter produce a good number of shoots or branches. Because these lazy bloomers are constantly passed from one cactus lover to another, we have many of them, like some of the different varieties from the genus *Echinopsis*.

Most of the cacti offered by nurseries and specialty stores bloom easily and willingly. These are cacti from the genera *Mammillaria*, *Notocactus*, *Echinopsis*, or *Rebutia*. If these eager bloomers refuse to produce flowers, it's usually because of the care they get. Most of the time, a necessary rest period is not provided. Almost all cacti will bloom only if they've been given a definite change to cooler and totally dry conditions during the winter months. For spring-flowering cacti, the rest period should last until flower buds are clearly visible. If they're watered too early, active growth begins and flower buds will not develop. Only after the flower buds have reached a certain size should you begin watering.

During the growing period, sufficient watering and fertilization are imperative. Cacti planted in a substrate (like sand or gravel) without nutrients that are seldom watered and never fertilized cannot produce flowers. Fertilizer rich in nitrogen supports growth but doesn't encourage flowering.

Some of the early-blooming cacti (some of the *Mammillaria*, *Rebutia*, or *Echinopsis*) can only produce flower buds if they haven't been deprived of light during the winter months. It's often difficult to find a place during the rest period that's cool *and* well lit. A windowsill on a cool staircase or a cool bedroom would be appropriate places that meet the criteria just mentioned.

Most cacti start to flower with the increase in daylight. Some species, however, do so when daylight decreases, like the *Mammillaria plumosa*, those of the *Rhipsalis* family, or the well-known Christmas cacti.

As soon as a cactus begins to produce flower buds, its exposure to light shouldn't be changed. Christmas and Easter cacti, for instance, will lose their buds if the direction of the light they receive is changed. Mark (with a pencil) the side of the pot that faces the light to avoid accidental changes.

Care During the Year

The following provides a schedule for the care of cacti during the course of a year. The seasons mentioned may vary somewhat depending on the climate (milder or harsher weather), and if the cacti are kept in a warm and sunny place, or in a cooler place.

EARLY SPRING

This is the best time for repotting, because the soil is dry. Early bloomers will show flower buds. The first to bloom are *Notocactus haselbergii* and the early-flowering *Mammillaria*, like *Mammillaria bombycina*, or *M. microhelia*. Cacti should be slowly introduced to moisture. In the beginning, water only occasionally, and more often when the plant begins to develop new branches or shoots. Burn injuries may occur during the first warm, sunny spring days. If necessary, the plants can be protected by shading them with tissue paper. In areas where the climate is favorable, hardy cacti able to withstand light frost when in the dry phase (like some *Echinocereus* cacti), may be placed in a hotbed by the second week of spring. Cacti seeds can be planted at this time on a warm windowsill, particularly if mild heat can be applied from below the container.

SPRING

Many cacti are now in full bloom, like those of the *Aporocactus*, *Echinocereus*, *Echinofossulocactus*, *Lobivia*, *Mammillaria*, *Rebutia*, and *Sulcorebutia* genera, as well as *Phyllocacti*. Water the cacti generously and begin to fertilize in midspring. This is a good time to start seeds, and to cut and to begin rooting cuttings. Cacti showing no sign of growth are most likely in trouble and should be taken out of their pots and inspected.

Move cacti in midspring from their winter locations, either to a ledge in front of a window, or outdoors. During the first few days, be sure that the surface tissue of these plants doesn't burn, because the plants aren't yet used to the intense light outside.

SUMMER

This is the time when the summer-flowering cacti are in their full glory: *Gymnocalycia*, *Notocactus*, *Parodia*, and *Coryphantha*, as well as many of the hybrids, like *Astrophytum* and *Echinopsis*.

Spring-flowering cacti have finished blooming and require a short rest period during the hot summer months. Watering should be reduced slightly. Seedlings need to be hardened now.

AUTUMN

Now the autumn-flowering cacti are in bloom, like the *Mammillaria gracilis* and *M. rhodantha*, and particularly those from the genus *Neoporteria*, as well as plants that have an extended flowering period, like *Astrophytum*, *Coryphantha*, *Parodia*, *Thelocactus*, and *Ferocactus setispinus*. For most cacti, the growing period is coming to a close. This means no more fertilizing, or, at most, a weak application of potassium-phosphorus fertilizer. This is also the time to open the windows of the hotbed, weather permitting, to harden plants with lots of fresh air and sunlight that isn't filtered through glass. Watering is reduced, from the beginning of autumn, for two to four weeks. After that, and through the beginning of winter, watering is almost totally discontinued. Starting in midautumn, all cacti on the window ledge outside and those in the hotbed must be moved inside.

WINTER

Only a few winter-flowering plants are still in bloom. But the time is near for cacti of the genus *Rhipsalis* and the Christmas cactus to bloom. Epiphytic plants need to be kept warm and moist. All other cacti are now in their rest period and should be kept dry and cool. Winter is the perfect time to study and explore subject-related literature, make notes, write down some of the observations made, and sort out slides taken during the summer.

Cacti Grouped by the Care They Need

Advice concerning the care of cacti seems very confusing at first. Most cacti, however, fit a particular category based on the care they need. Of course, there are always exceptions, but it seems that whole groups of cacti (even those that need special attention) have very

Mammillaria wood-sii, showing a typical ring of flowers

similar needs. What follows is a discussion of cactus care. The instructions about the needs of the individual types or species are divided into "Care Groups," with specifics mentioned when applicable.

CARE GROUP 1: STANDARD CARE

This group includes almost all cacti that have been discussed so far. This group includes all cacti of the genera *Mammillaria*, *Notocactus*, *Parodia*, *Gymnocalycium*, and *Echinofossulocactus*.

This group needs a sunny and well-lit location. Only those cacti with a green appearance and sparse spines need protection from direct, harsh, and hot sunlight. Temperatures during the summer months should be between 77 and 95 °F (25–35 °C), in the winter between 44 and 50 °F (6–10 °C). During their active growing season, the six months from midspring to midautumn, watering should be thorough and should be done every eighth or tenth day. During the winter months, however, water only very sparingly, since these cacti need to be kept dry.

40

The amount of moisture necessary in the winter depends upon the temperature. Water less when the plant is in a cooler location, water more when the plant is in a warmer location. These cacti thrive best in a southeast window, less so in a hot south-facing window.

CARE GROUP 2: SEMIDESERT CACTI NEEDING LOTS OF HEAT AND SUNSHINE

Cacti of this group are easily recognized by their "white" appearance. They have a white, frosty coat or strong, white or colored spination. All of these features indicate that they have adapted to direct sunlight and hot temperatures. Many of the "white" *Mammillaria* and most cacti belonging to the genera *Echinocereus*, *Astrophytum*, *Thelocactus*,

Ferocactus, and *Opuntia* belong to this group. These plants like full sun in the summer, with temperatures up to 113 °F (45 °C). South-facing windows or bay windows receiving full sun are ideal locations for this group. During the winter months, many of these plants (like *Echinocereus*) tolerate cooler temperatures, while others (like *Ferocactus*) shouldn't be exposed to temperatures lower than 54 °F (12 °C).

CARE GROUP 3: VIGOROUSLY GROWING CACTI FROM LOW-LYING REGIONS

Some cacti come from regions with a considerable amount of rainfall and fertile soil. They don't do well with little water and sterile soil. They're known for their vigorous growth. Many column

Echinofossulocactus crispatus. Echinofossulocacti have many lamellate, zigzagging ribs.

41

cacti, such as the well-known *Cereus peruvianus* and also those from the genera *Cleistocactus*, *Pilosocereus*, and *Selenicereus*, as well as some of the *Phyllocacti* that come from low-lying areas, belong to this group. These plants like a lot of light but not necessarily direct, full sun. They like rich, humus soil and frequent watering. Fertilization can be stronger than is customary for other cacti. They also tolerate (even like) winter temperatures up to 68 °F (20 °C).

Watering should be decreased during the winter, but not eliminated.

CARE GROUP 4: CACTI FROM HIGHER REGIONS THAT LOVE FRESH AIR

These cacti come from high, mountainous regions. They like lots of light and fresh air, but they won't tolerate high temperatures. They do like temperature extremes between day and

Phyllocacti. **These cacti have been well known for a long time, and wonderful hybrids have been developed.**

**Above: "Climax"
Below: "High Fashion"**

night, and between summer and winter. Cacti in this group belong to the genera *Lobivia, Rebutia, Sulcorebutia, Oreocereus* and others, as well as those *Echinopsis* cacti that grow in high regions (*Pseudolobivia*). These plants do poorly behind a hot, south-facing window, but they do wonderfully in a well-ventilated hotbed or on a ledge in front of a window, if sufficient protection from rain can be provided. Southeast and southwest windows are also fine if sufficient fresh air is provided. Sunlight in higher regions includes a high content of ultraviolet rays. Since ultraviolet light does not penetrate window glass, these cacti appreciate direct sunlight at least now and then. During the winter months, all watering should cease and temperatures shouldn't exceed 40–43 °F (4–6 °C). If planted in dry sand, these cacti will even tolerate short, light frost during the night. Rank and unsightly growth will occur if they are kept in a warm location during the winter, and flower buds will develop only sparsely.

CARE GROUP 5: EPIPHYTIC CACTI

These cacti come from tropical forests. The care they need is very different from that needed for other cacti. Their care is much like the care for orchids, which come from the same region. Included here are cacti from the genus *Rhipsalis*, as well as Easter and Christmas cacti, and many *Phyllocacti*. They need a humus and porous soil, and the plants must be continuously moist. The root system should never dry out completely. In addition, these cacti need a certain amount of humidity. The plants like light, but not full sun. Good locations, therefore, are windows facing north, northwest, or northeast, or bay windows. Provide some time outdoors in the shade of a bush or a tree.

PROPAGATING CACTI

Cacti can be propagated by seeds and—often simpler—by rooting cuttings.

Propagation by Seed

It's not particularly difficult to grow cacti from seed. Cactus seeds germinate very slowly, and even small seedlings will grow slowly. Although cacti seedlings need moisture for germination, they are susceptible to fungus infection. Therefore, it's necessary to provide proper warmth and moisture, but attempts should be made to prevent fungus infection.

Phyllocactus with a large berry

Growing cacti from seeds in large quantities or trying to grow those cacti that are known to have a particularly difficult, slow germination period, and those cacti whose seeds sometimes may look like dust, ought to be left to experienced gardeners.

The beginner *can* find suitable species for seed propagation (like column cacti), and only a few simple aids are needed. Growing from seed allows the gardener to make many interesting observations. A plant grown from seed represents a very special experience, providing the gardener with a very special relationship to that plant. Here are a few tips on how to grow cacti seeds.

CACTI SEEDS

The specialist offers a great variety of seeds. The beginner should choose for his first attempt either a mixture of several different types of seed, or he should use column-cacti seeds that grow vigorously, or he could choose seeds from cacti that bloom after only a few years, like those of the genus *Rebutia*. Of course, it's fine to use seeds that were given by a friend. However, seeds should not be older than one or two years. Before planting, care should be taken that every trace of pulp is removed from every seed to prevent the development of fungus. Put larger seeds in a tea sieve and smaller seeds in a cloth bag, and, submerging them in warm water, wash them carefully and gently. Afterwards dry them on a paper towel.

CONTAINERS AND SOIL FOR SOWING SEEDS

Shallow, small pots, dishes used for dish gardens, and Styrofoam dishes are all good for sowing seeds. Containers should be cleaned well with hot water before filling them with soil. Provide drainage holes (Styrofoam can easily be punctured with a pencil), and cover the holes with pieces of broken clay pots. Now fill the container two-thirds full with cactus soil. The soil should be very porous and it should contain a substantial amount of coarse sand and perlite. Heat the soil to disinfect it. This protects against possible fungus infection, but it's not absolutely necessary. Cover the cactus soil with a ¼″ (0.5 cm) layer of brick pebbles, lava sand, or ordinary coarse sand. Clean such material first by putting it in a sieve that only lets pebbles that are about ¹⁄₁₆″ (1 to 2 mm) in diameter pass through. Clean the material under running water to remove dust and mud, dry it, and then spread it over the soil. This layer has no nutritional value and merely functions to prevent the growth of bacteria.

SEEDBED CONTAINER

Seeds will germinate particularly well in most containers if you can provide temperatures of 68–77 °F (20–25 °C). An overnight temperature of about 60 °F (15 °C) is very beneficial; however, temperatures lower than this, and those higher than 98 °F (35 °C), might delay or prevent germination. The necessary temperature can be achieved if the seedbed is covered by a plastic dome and a heating cable is placed under the box. Such covered seedbeds are equipped with a thermostat that regulates the temperature automatically. This is only necessary if the temperature outside the seedbed fluctuates drastically. The addition of a heating element isn't necessary if the seedbed is located in heated living quarters. One such spot would be a windowsill over a radiator, where a constant temperature is maintained. Increase and maintain the humidity by closing the top of the seedbed. A well-lit location is necessary, since cacti need light to germinate. A windowsill that faces north or east is ideal. Don't expose the seedbed to direct sunlight. This eliminates the choice of south- or west-facing windows. Direct sunlight increases temperatures dramatically in such a location. Light is needed for germination to take place, but not blazing sun.

SOWING SEEDS

Cacti seeds need to be spread evenly over the soil.

Fold a piece of paper in half, and by gently tapping, the seeds will glide (one at a time) along the crease and then fall onto the soil. Since cacti seeds take a considerable amount of time to germinate and since they all like company, sow the seeds densely. As a guide, spread about 20 cacti seeds evenly over a space of about ¾" × ¾" (2 × 2 cm).

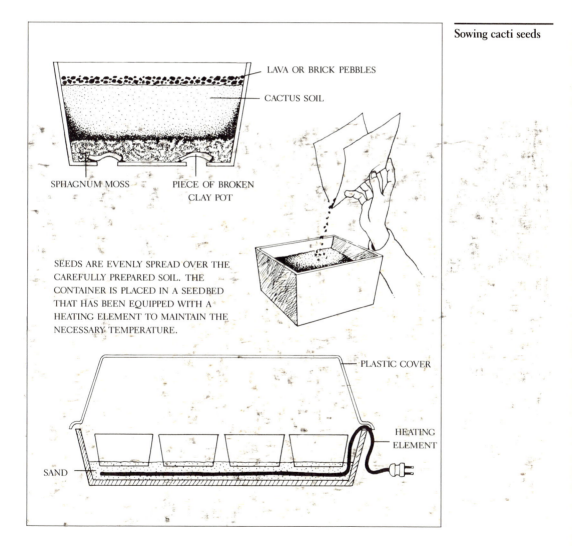

LAVA OR BRICK PEBBLES

CACTUS SOIL

SPHAGNUM MOSS

PIECE OF BROKEN CLAY POT

SEEDS ARE EVENLY SPREAD OVER THE CAREFULLY PREPARED SOIL. THE CONTAINER IS PLACED IN A SEEDBED THAT HAS BEEN EQUIPPED WITH A HEATING ELEMENT TO MAINTAIN THE NECESSARY TEMPERATURE.

PLASTIC COVER

HEATING ELEMENT

SAND

After the seeds have been spread out, use a flat object, like a piece of cardboard, and gently press the seeds into the soil. Since cacti seeds need light for germination, the seeds shouldn't be covered.

Seeds and soil should now be moistened. Don't use a watering can for this purpose, since so much water would dislocate the seeds in the soil. Setting the pots in a dish of water until the soil is well moistened from below is a much better method. Add a mild solution of potassium hydroxyquinoline sulphate to the water to prevent fungus. This additive is a mild disinfectant. Now set the pots into the seedbed "house" and close the cover to retain moisture in the soil and humidity in the seedbed.

Gymnocalycium gibbosum **grows podlike fruits that burst open unevenly.**

GERMINATION

During germination the soil must not dry out. Use a thermometer to check on the temperature. Many cacti seeds germinate within a two-week period. It's interesting to watch the seed shell open and to see the two small cotyledons develop, from which the body of the cactus will develop in turn. When most of the seeds have germinated, raise the cover of the seedbed to lower the humidity inside and thereby lessen the chance of fungus infection. After about three to four months, the individual pots can be removed from the seedbed. Move them to a location that's well lit and provides some sunlight, but not full sun. Even in nature, cacti seedlings

grow in the shadow of mature cacti or other vegetation.

It's best for seedlings to remain in the pots where they've been sown. The soil can now become a little dryer, but seedlings do need more water than mature cacti, since the soil is more porous and roots are still very immature. Continue to water from the bottom to ensure that the seedlings grow into healthy plants. To ensure proper acidic conditions in the soil, add potassium and phosphate to the water (approximately ¼ teaspoon [1 g] of potassium-phosphate to 2 quarts [2 litres] of water).

TRANSPLANTING

As soon as seedlings have grown to the point where they've formed a solid cushion, they must be transplanted into fresh soil. This should be done when the soil in the seed pot is dry, so that seedlings won't be harmed. Seedlings are now about ¼" (0.5 cm) in diameter, and they should be planted—not individually but several together—in larger pots or dishes. The soil in the new container should have normal porous structure and be rather dry. Use a piece of wood or a pencil to make holes, one for each seedling. Gently and carefully push soil around the seedling. The distance between each seedling should be three times the size of one seedling.

After transplanting, find a warm but shaded place for the seedlings. Watering should be suspended for two days until injuries sustained during the transplanting have healed. Water very gently. After the seedlings have established themselves well (approximately one week later) they can be moved to a partially shaded location. The plants are now

Cacti seedlings

49

able to grow rather briskly and without any problems.

SOWING SEEDS IN A CLOSED PLASTIC BAG

Some cacti lovers have great luck with an uncomplicated method of growing cacti from seed. Containers are prepared and filled as described in the previous chapter. With this method, however, the soil is much more vigorously sterilized and the top layer consists of *sterile* sand, perlite, or pumice. The seeds are spread over the soil as described previously and receive a generous amount of water, from the bottom. Add potassium hydroxyquinoline sulphate to the water to prevent fungus. After excess water has drained from the soil, the pots are placed in an airtight plastic bag (without holes) and are either set down or suspended from the ceiling in a well-lit location without direct sunlight. Because no moisture can escape, these seedbeds need very little attention and care, often for up to 3 months. Success depends upon on how well you prevent fungus.

After three to four months, the container is removed from the plastic bag and the seedlings are transplanted exactly as described previously. This problem-free method is worth a try, particularly if you have lots of seeds.

Propagation from Cuttings

Propagating cacti from cuttings is simple, and in most cases successful. Cuttings for rooting are best taken during the active growing period in spring and summer. With a sharp knife (not serrated), portions are cut off from the mother cactus. Try to minimize injury to the mother. In general, such cuttings don't need any special attention. Some-times the mother plant has already produced offsets that have developed roots while they're still attached. If a head that has been cut off from a column cactus is to be rooted, bevel the cutting surface so that new roots will grow in the middle, from the deepest point. Cuttings from a leaf cactus (*Phyllocactus*) are usually made at the base of the leaf on the mother plant. However, the leaf is usually very tough there, and does not develop roots easily. A cutting taken from the base of a *Phyllocactus* is, therefore, recut at the wider portion of the leaf. See the illustration on page 50.

Cacti cuttings are not rooted in water like those of fuchsia plants, for example. The cutting surface of a cactus is properly dried to prevent bacteria from entering the plant. If the cutting surface is small, and injury to already developing roots is also small, the cutting is left to dry for a week. If injuries are more extensive, the cuttings might have to be dried for up to three months. During this time, the cuttings must be kept upright, since roots develop according to gravity. A *Cereus* cutting, therefore, must be kept upright, perhaps suspended in a sling, or set upright in a clay pot with other cuttings for support, and allowed to dry. A cutting left on its side will develop roots all along its underside.

If the cutting surfaces have sufficiently dried and new root tips are visible, gently plant the cuttings in relatively porous soil. Spray just in the beginning, rather than regularly. Water until enough suction roots have developed.

If the cut-off top portion of a truncated column cactus has rooted vigorously, growth can be initiated by adding a good amount of fertilizer to the planting soil. The cutting surface should not

The truncated top of a *Trichocereus* hybrid, showing new shoots

The shoot from the truncated cactus was cut off and allowed to dry. Here it shows newly developed roots.

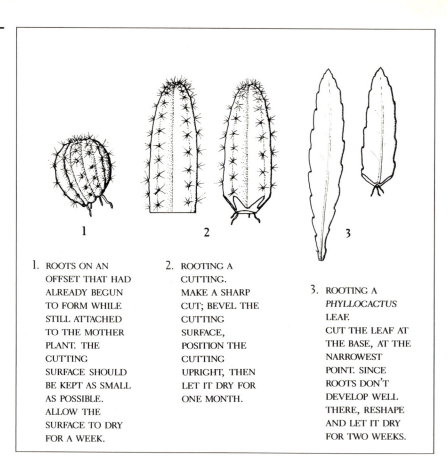

1. ROOTS ON AN OFFSET THAT HAD ALREADY BEGUN TO FORM WHILE STILL ATTACHED TO THE MOTHER PLANT. THE CUTTING SURFACE SHOULD BE KEPT AS SMALL AS POSSIBLE. ALLOW THE SURFACE TO DRY FOR A WEEK.

2. ROOTING A CUTTING. MAKE A SHARP CUT; BEVEL THE CUTTING SURFACE, POSITION THE CUTTING UPRIGHT, THEN LET IT DRY FOR ONE MONTH.

3. ROOTING A *PHYLLOCACTUS* LEAF. CUT THE LEAF AT THE BASE, AT THE NARROWEST POINT. SINCE ROOTS DON'T DEVELOP WELL THERE, RESHAPE AND LET IT DRY FOR TWO WEEKS.

become wet during the drying period. In a few weeks the mother cactus will develop new shoots from the areoles at the side. These shoots can also be cut off and rooted as soon as they've reached a sufficient size. You can thus increase the number of plants easily.

The growth rate of small cuttings can be increased by grafting them to an already growing base. A *Trichocereus* is a good example. Experts will graft a small seedling onto an appropriate base. Particularly favored are cacti from the genus *Pereskiopsis*.

DISEASES AND PESTS

Given the proper basic care, cacti are robust and hardy plants. Hardened and properly cultivated cacti are very seldom attacked by pests or diseases. Cacti that are insufficiently hardened and have gone through an excessive, rapid growth period are often very susceptible to pest damage. The best protection, therefore, is proper care. Even with the most diligent care, however, pests and disease can attack a plant.

Damage Due to Improper Care

Most damage to cacti is caused by improper care. Some of the typical signs of damage are listed below.

CACTI REMAIN SMALL, AND SHOW WEAK, "LEGGY" GROWTH

If otherwise low-growing, upright, and firm cacti suddenly start to grow rapidly, to the point where they need to be supported and their otherwise dark green color turns yellow-green, you have a sure sign that the plant isn't receiving enough light. This often happens, for instance, with *Opuntia* cuttings that have been placed in a dark living-room window. These plants need to be moved to a well-lit area, and a more appropriate plant should be found for such a location. The same symptoms may indicate that the nitrogen content either in the fertilizer or in the soil is too high. In addition, the same symptoms will appear if a cactus has been forced into an active growing period during the winter by being placed in a location that's too warm, and the plant has received too much water. In such a situation, the gardener must make sure that the necessary rest period is strictly adhered to.

WHITE-TO-YELLOW SPOTS

Yellow or white spots on the ridge, and on the side of the cactus facing the sun, are due to damage of the surface tissue caused by too much heat and direct sunlight. Cacti gardeners call these spots "burns."

These burns usually happen during the first bright and sunny spring days that follow a long, drab winter. The danger of "burning" is particularly great for a cactus in a south-facing window. Such damage can disfigure a cactus for many years. The gardener should make sure that during the very first sunny spring days the plant is properly shaded. Cover the cacti with tissue paper during the hours of strong sunlight. Fresh air will also help to dissipate accumulated heat.

REDDISH DISCOLORATION ON THE BODY OF THE CACTUS

Reddish discoloration is an indication that the plant is under stress. This can happen if the cactus (because light and temperature have increased) is trying to grow actively, but is prevented due to lack of water. The same discoloration can occur if a cactus has been moved to an unheated hotbed where temperatures are still rather low. This discoloration will normally disappear as the environment improves, and when the cactus continues its normal growth.

Some cacti native to high elevations, like the highland *Echinopsis* from the group of *Pseudolobivia*, or the *Lobivia*

Burns on the surface tissue of a *Gymnocalycium*, caused by sudden, direct, strong sunlight.

(*Chamaecereus*) *silvestri*, do normally change to a (more or less) strong red color in the spring. The coloration of these plants is no reason for concern.

YELLOW DISCOLORATION OF THE WHOLE OR PARTS OF A CACTUS (CHLOROSIS)

The whole cactus or individual segments will turn yellow if its mineral composition is out of balance. Minerals or trace minerals like iron may not be present in sufficient amounts. Or—and this is usually the case—nutrition that is present cannot reach the plant for two reasons: the pH value has become too high (alkalinization), or too much lime has accumulated in the soil. A plant damaged for these reasons is best repotted in fresh soil.

In such cases, completely remove the old soil. Since injuries are impossible to prevent during repotting, suspend watering for a few days and move the plant to a partially shaded location.

"CORKING" STARTING AT THE BASE OF THE PLANT

Unsightly brown spots and splotches, starting at the base of a cactus, usually happen when the care given to the cactus is very irregular. Such "corking" begins when the cactus receives irregular watering; often the water used is too cold, or it has poorly balanced fertilizer or nutrition. Such discoloration is not uncommon among some cacti like *Astrophytum*, *Echinopsis*, or *Trichocereus*, and can't be prevented.

54

"Corking" of a
Trichocereus

Fungus infection on
the surface tissue of
an *Echinopsis ferox*.
The plant was able
to isolate the
infection.

LOST OR "STUCK" FLOWER BUDS

If a bud doesn't open or if it falls off, it's because the plant has been moved from the direction from which it received light when it first developed. This condition has been reported with Christmas cacti. Perhaps the amount of light, moisture, and nutrition, and the degree of warmth, are insufficient for the bud to mature. A change in the weather might be the reason, or the gardener has gone on vacation. However, many cacti produce more buds than will later go into full bloom.

Fungus Infections

Cacti usually come from dry climates. The mineral-rich soil in their native habitats was created over time from layers of disintegrated rock. Cacti are somewhat sensitive to fungus infections. If injuries don't have a chance to heal, and if the cactus is potted in damp, warm, humus soil, the all-pervasive presence of bacteria will penetrate the unstable, exposed cells at the site of the injury, and rot may set in rather quickly.

It's very difficult to treat fungus infections. The so-called fungicides can't totally destroy the bacteria and their spores; they're only able to inhibit the infection for a short time. The best protection against such infections is prevention. The experienced gardener will choose a porous, mineral-rich soil. If a cactus whose native climate is dry has tuberlike roots, it should be set in soil that's particularly porous and contains a sufficient amount of sand. This type of cactus needs protection around the upper part of the root and the base of the plant. Every cactus (including seedlings) should be potted (or repotted) in rather dry soil and only watered after a few days have passed and injuries have had a chance to heal. Cuttings must be air-dried and allowed to complete callousing on the cutting surface before they're set into the soil and watered. Cacti should not be kept in places where the air is stagnant and humid, but rather in an environment with lots of fresh air.

Cacti can be infected by many different fungi, and sometimes only a specialist can distinguish among them. Almost all infections mean that the plant is lost. If a whole section of cacti seedlings suddenly turns transparent and falls over (which can sometimes happen overnight), discard the whole section. Those seedlings that have not been affected should be sprayed with a mild solution of potassium hydroxyquinoline sulphate. The humidity for the remaining seedlings should be reduced and they should be kept rather dry. If a mature cactus becomes mushy and falls over, discard the whole plant immediately; even its pot should not be reused until it has been scrubbed with boiling water.

One might be tempted to think that a cactus infected at the base is still healthy at its upper part. It's possible to cut off the upper part (high in the healthy area) with a knife disinfected in alcohol and to allow the cutting to reroot. But it may become clear that bacteria has already spread into the portion of the plant that still seems to be healthy, and that rot will continue to spread.

Caution is advised if black spots suddenly appear on the surface of a cactus, particularly near the ribs. These spots can be absolutely harmless, but they can also be evidence of a dangerous and rapidly spreading fungus infection. It is best to immediately move the affected plant to an isolated, dry location and keep a close watch. Do the spots dry up or are they spreading? Such infections usually happen during the warm season when cacti (in the greenhouse) are sprayed with water and then remain in the humid air due to inadequate ventilation.

Pests

Robust, hardy cacti, cared for as nature intended, are less likely to be attacked by pests than those cacti that have been pampered, whose growth has been forced, or which have been exposed to unfavorable conditions. An infestation of pests can affect even healthy plants. Such pests usually arrive when an unsuspecting gardener adds an infected cactus to his collection. Inspect "new arrivals" very carefully, whether you bought them at a store or received them as gifts, and then quarantine the plants for a few days.

MEALYBUGS

White to light grey spots spread unevenly over the surface of a cactus are an indication of a heavy infestation of mealybugs. The insects reach a length of $\frac{3}{16}''$ (4 mm), and they're protected by excreting a whitish, mealy wax. They usually hide between narrow ribs, between the mother plant and her offsets, or at the points where grafting has been done. These bugs wander over the plant with great speed and lay their eggs, which are also protected by the waxlike threads. They weaken the plant by sucking its juice. Since pesticides cannot penetrate their protective wax layer, chemical treatment is not easy. If the number of affected plants is small, you can pick the bugs off one by one, using a swab (or a fine brush) dipped in alcohol. It's important that you maintain a daily treatment over several weeks, since hidden eggs continue to hatch. If you choose chemical pesticide treatment, use something that's specifically designed to kill mealybugs. A wide-spectrum pesticide can also be used. However, wide-spectrum pesticides will also affect the blue or white frosting of some cacti.

SCALE

These pests are sometimes observed on leaf cacti, *Opuntia*, or column cacti and look like small, slightly raised brown spots. Mature bugs live under a protective shield that doesn't move. The female bug lays its eggs under this shield and the young scale hatch there. Here again, pesticides do not penetrate the protective shield, and a treatment with a swab dipped in alcohol is best. In the course of this treatment be careful not to spread the eggs and the immature bugs all over the plant. Dab or spray the spot with pesticide where the scale has been removed. Daily treatment must be kept up for a few weeks and close inspection is necessary to catch unhatched and newly hatched eggs. *Phyllocacti*, however, may show small brown spots that might be a form of harmless "corking." If that's the case, don't treat the spots.

ROOT MEALYBUGS

These pests live on and in the cactus root system and grow to a length of $\frac{1}{12}''$ (2 mm). Chalky white spots are immediately visible during repotting. Root mealybugs multiply fast and spread throughout a cacti collection rapidly, and not just outdoors; they also crawl from one pot's drainage hole to another's. They multiply particularly fast during the dry rest period when plants don't get much attention. Roots are weakened due to the pest's sucking. Cacti infected with these bugs begin to lose their healthy green appearance and will not produce strong new offsets and flower buds. Root mealybugs are found in many cacti collections, including those in many nurseries. Closely inspect and repot new arrivals immediately. If a plant is indeed infected, remove all of the soil and thoroughly clean the entire root system. The pot the cactus came in must be thoroughly disinfected. In addition, the plant must be watered at least twice within a span of ten days.

NEMATODES

Cacti can be infested with nematodes in either of two ways. First, they may form galls in the root system. Young nematodes are released from these galls; then they bore into the roots and continue to form more galls. Or, cyst-building nematodes may infest the plant. The body of the female swells up like a bladder, and she produces lemon-shaped, yellow-to-brown cysts $\frac{1}{48}''$ (0.5 mm) in size. These cysts protect the young larvae. Sometimes they won't leave the cyst for years, and then they'll begin to attack the roots again.

The first sign of nematode infection is disruption of growth. Only later will the root system deteriorate, causing the infected cactus to die. Nematodes are usually detected rather late, and other plants may already have been infected, sometimes by the reuse of old soil. A suspicious plant must be repotted and inspected.

A sure sign of nematode infection is decay of the root system. Sometimes an irregular "broom" webbing of new roots is present. If such is the case, submerge the root system in water and remove all the soil. Inspect the surface of the water using a magnifying glass. If the roots are infected, it's easy to detect the smooth, lemon-shaped, brownish yellow nematode cysts floating on the water surface, and on the soil particles that are now also floating on the water surface.

Nematodes are very hard to kill. Standard pesticide solutions are only able to kill living nematodes, but the many cysts will release young ones for years. Pesticides that kill nematodes are available, but they're extremely poisonous and they're not sold to home gardeners. If a plant is infected with nematodes, cut off the root system drastically. The root stump should be thoroughly cleaned and the plant should be left to air-dry. The dried cutting surface is then grafted onto another plant. Soil left over from the old pot should not be reused for repotting.

RED SPIDER MITES

These reddish- or yellowish-colored animals are so small that they can only be seen through a magnifying glass. They suck juices from the tissues of new growth, they weaken the plant, and they multiply rapidly. The parts of the plant that are infected look scabby and show a pale, yellowish white discoloration. Sometimes it's possible with the aid of a magnifying glass to detect a fine webbing of spider mites.

Tissue destroyed by red spider mites won't regenerate; the plant will be disfigured for years, and will die if the infection is severe. Spider mites are also common on other plants, and preventing an infection is often impossible.

Some cacti, like *Lobivia silvestrii* (particularly those that have been grafted on top of a host plant), and the *Echinocereus* with its soft tissue, and all plants that have been pampered and not sufficiently hardened, are particularly susceptible. Infected plants must be thoroughly sprayed with the appropriate pesticide, saturating all the crevices on the plant. Treatment should be done several times in approximately 10-day intervals in order to catch all the young hatchlings. Severely infected plants should be isolated from the other plants. Eventually, the spider mites' ability to multiply rapidly also makes them resistant to the pesticide that's being used.

OTHER PESTS

Snails often invade a hotbed and can cause major damage. They particularly like to feed on *Phyllocacti*. The presence of snails can be detected by their slimy tracks. During the day, snails usually hide under pots and dishes; a thorough search is necessary to find them. Specialty stores offer specific snail bait.

Wood lice (pill bugs, sow bugs) can also cause major damage with their feeding habits. Trap them in potatoes that you've cut in half and hollowed out. These pests like to retreat into potatoes during the day.

Springtails (collembolans) are sometimes found in epiphytic cacti; they can be removed using a pesticide spray.

Pesticides

Some pesticides offered in small quantities by nurseries are suitable for gardeners with only a small collection of

A *Rebutia*, showing the damage caused by red spider mites

cacti. In many countries pesticides containing the same ingredients are often marketed under different names. Furthermore, the number and kind of approved pesticides for sale vary greatly. Obtain more detailed information from trained personnel in specialty stores and from appropriate regulatory agencies.

Some pesticides are poisonous to humans and animals. Manufacturers' instructions for dosages and application must be closely followed. Some pesticides damage the plant being treated; it seems that epiphytic plants, like Christmas and Easter cacti, are more sensitive than other cacti. If in doubt, get detailed information and advice from trained specialists or regulatory agencies. An intensive application of pesticides should be done during the warm season and not in the winter when the cactus root system is dry. Plants that have been sprayed with insecticides must be moved to a shaded location for several days; direct exposure to sun immediately after treatment can cause serious damage to the plant. To avoid damage, the distance between the plant and the spray can should be at least 12"–20" (30–50 cm).

Remember, too, that pesticides pose health risks even after you're done using them. Empty pesticide containers *must* be disposed of properly. Many communities require that you separate toxic substances from your "regular" garbage, and you may even be forced to make a special trip to a collection site intended for toxic waste. Many pesticides are harmful to groundwater, septic systems and city sewage systems. Don't pour leftover pesticides down your drains, and this same warning also applies to paints, solvents, cleaning fluids, and a host of other substances. Your local community should be able to give you instructions for the disposal of these substances.

Pesticides should be stored out of reach of children and pets. In addition to the danger of accidental poisoning and environmental contamination, there's also a risk of fire and explosion. Follow the manufacturers' instructions regarding the storage and disposal of pesticides.

RECOMMENDED CACTI FROM DIFFERENT GENERA AND VARIETIES

In this chapter we've selected for discussion different genera and varieties of cactus that we feel are particularly beautiful. Of course, cacti lovers have their own convictions about which cactus is the most beautiful. We chose those that are considered of prime beauty, that are suitable for a small collection, that do well either in a window or in a hotbed, and that are easily available in specialty stores and nurseries.

Recognizing a particular cactus is not all that easy, since cacti are cultivated from more than 2,000 varieties. Even experts have trouble properly identifying a cactus when it's not in bloom. Several types of cactus have definite characteristics that we've listed specifically with a general description of the cactus.

Identifying characteristics alone for specific varieties aren't enough, given the great number of different genera we're dealing with. Identifying cacti, however, is definitely not a matter of counting spines (they vary greatly). Unfortunately, many cacti on the market are mislabelled, or are listed by only one of several names by which a cactus is known.

The first criterion for identifying a cactus is its shape. The table on page 63 lists only those cacti included in this book.

Aporocactus

Characteristic of this plant are its long, thin, trailing pendant branches, which may grow between 7 and 12 ribs. It can be distinguished from other rattail cacti by its large red flower that opens during the day. This genus consists of only a few varieties, and it's difficult to distinguish among them.

APOROCACTUS FLAGELLIFORMIS (RATTAIL CACTUS)

The double-sided, symmetrical (*zygomorphic*) flower is very similar to that of the Christmas cactus. This cactus has been cultivated as a houseplant for nearly 300 years. As its common name implies, it's well known to those who aren't necessarily cactus lovers. The rattail cactus, blooming profusely, can be found on balconies and on windowsills among many other hardy houseplants. This cactus is widely dispersed throughout the tropics, and it's difficult to trace its origin. It's said to have originated in the state of Hidalgo in Mexico, where the *Aporocactus flagelliformis* grows on host trees, and, in areas where the humidity is higher, it also trails down from rock formations.

When cultivating this cactus at home, consider its semi-epiphytic way of life. A porous soil substrate should be mixed with regular potting soil, perlite, sand, and, perhaps, some sphagnum moss.

During winter, maintain temperatures between 43 and 46 °F (6–8 °C), but these cacti also tolerate somewhat lower temperatures, though only for a short period. Because of its trailing pendant branches, this is an ideal hanging plant. During the warm season the plant needs bright, but not direct harsh

Color photo of *Aporocactus flagelliformis* can be found on page 33.

61

sunlight. It also does well outside in partial shade under a tree and protected from direct midday sun. Since this plant is prone to spider mite infections, it must be hardened well by providing fresh outside air.

APOROCACTUS HYBRIDS

Cacti of many different shapes can be successfully hybridized. The very beautiful *Aporocactus* hybrids are good examples.

As far back as 1830, the English horticulturist Mallison crossed the A. *flagelliformis* with the upright-growing *Heliocereus*. The result was the well-known *Aporocactus mallisonii* with large bright-red flowers, 4"–6" (10–15 cm) in length. During the 1950s, a breeder from Germany produced an exciting hybrid between A. *flagelliformis* and *Trichocereus candicans*.

Aporophyllum. The name of these hybrids represents a combination of *Aporocactus* and *Epiphyllum* (*Phyllocacti*).

Lately, particularly in Great Britain, hybrids have been created between *Aporocacti* and *Phyllocacti* (*Epiphyllum* hybrids), resulting in greater variety in the size of the plant, having either more trailing or more arched branches, as well as many more beautiful colors; yellow is the only color missing at this point. Their names combine the names of both "parents"— *Aporophyllum* hybrids. Their care groups, according to their parents: 1, 3, or 5.

Astrophytum

Cacti from the *Astrophytum* variety usually have fewer ribs and a white woolly covering on their surface; they bring a sense of the exotic to a cacti collection.

A list of cacti organized by genus, with their most important characteristics.

Shapes of cacti

Type	Genus	Characteristics
Column cacti	*Browningia hertlingiana*	Blue "frosting"
	Cephalocereus	Grey hairs
	Cereus	Hairless blossom
	Cleistocactus	Flower without cilia
	Echinocereus	Green stigmas
	Espostoa	White- or grey-haired covering
	Eulychnia	Woolly areoles
	Haageocereus	(Often) colored spines
	Hildewintera	Short inner blossom leaves
	Oreocereus	White- or grey-haired covering
	Pilosocereus	Long and woolly areoles
	Setiechinopsis	Starlike flowers with very short petals
	Stetsonia	V-shaped ridge crossing the areoles
	Trichocereus	Circle of stigmas in the center
Rattail Cacti	*Aporocactus*	Red flowers, open during the day
	Selenicereus	Flowers open at night, 10″ (25 cm) tall
Barrel Cacti	*Astrophytum*	Woolly surface
	Echinocactus	Very large barrel cacti
	Echinofossulocactus	Lamella-like ribs
	Echinopsis	Center has a wreath of stamens. Relatively long tubelike flowers
	Ferocactus	(Often) flattened hooked spines or curly spines
	Gymnocalycium	Areoles with horizontal ridges; flowers with large, bald scales on the outside
	Lobivia	Center with a stigma circle and short tubelike flowers
	Neoporteria	Many different shapes
	Notocactus	Often red stigmas
	Parodia	Flower with heavy spine growth on the outside; (often) hooked spines
	Rebutia	Flowers develop sideways near the base
	Sulcorebutia	Comblike spines
	Thelocactus	Flowers are located at the end of a short furrow
	Turbinicarpus	Paperlike or feathery spines
True tubercle cacti (tubercles **and** flowers develop in the tubercles)	*Coryphantha*	Flowering tubercles, grooved
	Mammillaria	Tubercles not grooved

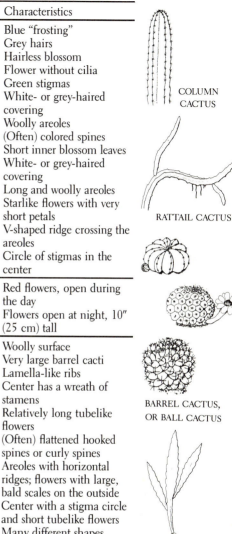

COLUMN CACTUS

RATTAIL CACTUS

BARREL CACTUS, OR BALL CACTUS

LEAF CACTUS

JOINTED AND UNJOINTED CACTUS (SEGMENTED LEAVES)

63

OPUNTIA
(SEGMENTED)

Type	Genus	Characteristics
Leaf cacti	*Phyllocacti*	Flowers more than ¾″ (2 cm) long
	Rhipsalis	Flowers up to ¾″ (2 cm) long
Cacti with jointed branches	*Rhipsalidopsis*	Flowers radially symmetrical
	Rhipsalis	Flowers up to ⅜″ (1 cm) in diameter
	Schlumbergera	Flowers doublesidedly symmetrical
Opuntiae	*Opuntia*	(Often) flat, leaflike pads

Color photo of an *Astrophytum* hybrid can be found on page 25.

They're native to the hot and dry regions of Texas and Mexico. Their ideal place is a sunny warm window. They prefer mineral-rich, porous soil, little watering and a dry rest period in winter with a temperature of 46 °F (8 °C.) Their seeds are big and germinate rather quickly. See Care Group 2.

ASTROPHYTUM CAPRICORNE

This variety stands out due to its irregular, long and brown spination and big yellow flowers with a deep red center. This plant tolerates temperatures lower than the other *Astrophytum* can stand.

Color photo of *Astrophytum myriostigma* can be found on page 12.

ASTROPHYTUM MYRIOSTIGMA

This is one of the few spineless cacti. It may or may not have white tufts, and it may have a different number of ribs. The plants with four ribs seem to be square. Flowering occurs when the plant is still rather small.

ASTROPHYTUM ORNATUM

In contrast to A. *capricorne*, this cactus has white feltlike spots arranged in a distinct pattern. Flowering doesn't occur until an advanced age. This is a rather decorative plant, due to its distinct pattern and its brown spines.

ASTROPHYTUM HYBRIDS

The first *Astrophytum* hybrids were produced in the 19th century. Crossbreeding between the many different varieties has led to the creation of a number of (more or less) flocked plants with (more or fewer) spines and with different ribs.

Browningia

BROWNINGIA HERTLINGIANA

These huge column cacti from South America are cultivated as young plants because of their beautiful blue frosty covering. This covering only develops in a warm climate and with much light, and the cactus must reach a height of at least 4″ to 6″ (10–15 cm). This plant requires very little watering and should not be exposed to water spray. See Care Group 3.

Cephalocereus

The only variety of this genus, *Cephalocereus senilis* from Mexico, can be identified by its long, trailing white hair, which covers its whole body. Another species from South America, belonging to the *Espostoa* group, is also totally covered with white hair. The hair of this last species isn't as bushy, but rather it covers its body more like a cocoon.

CEPHALOCEREUS SENILIS

These large column cacti are often bought as young plants because of their typical white hair. Keep them in a warm and well-lit location and water only sparingly. See Care Group 2.

Cereus

CEREUS PERUVIANUS

Cereus column cacti, often growing 13 feet (4 m) high, can sometimes be seen in large greenhouses, in botanical gardens, or in hotel lobbies, where they willingly display their yellowish white flowers. You may find that seeds that come as part of a seed mixture yield the rather monstrously shaped rock cactus. These young plants will need special nurturing. At the beginning of this century, this cactus was part of all respectable cacti collections. Some of its popularity has been lost in recent years. It does well, given the proper environment. Be careful that no insects nest in its folds and crevices. See Care Group 3.

Cleistocactus

These column cacti have very attractive spination. Some varieties will develop their beautiful, interestingly shaped flowers when the plant is only 8″–16″ (20–40 cm) high. The flowers are elongated, tubular, with dense scales on the outside, and sometimes trailing. They're pollinated by hummingbirds. Even a gardener with very little space can make room for a column cactus and enjoy its flowers. The plant should not

be placed in direct sunlight. During its active growth cycle, this plant needs plenty of fertilizer and sufficient water. See Care Group 3.

CLEISTOCACTUS RITTERI

White spines and yellow-green flowers amid long white hair that develops after the plant is 16″ (40 cm) high make this an interesting plant. It's easy to care for, so it's popular.

CLEISTOCACTUS SMARAGDIFLORUS

This variety carries flowers that are straight and red, with green edging. The plant will start (and continue) to bloom when it's only 10″ (25 cm) high. This plant shouldn't be kept too cold nor too dry during the winter months.

Cereus Peruvianus f. monstrosus. Normally this variety develops into a big column. This cactus, however, has developed cristate, inwardly projecting growth.

Color photo of *Cephalocereus senilis* can be found on page 23.

65

cactus and *Echinopsis*. These hybrids are called *Cleistopsis*, a combination of the parents' names. They're usually column-shaped, but the column is a little shorter and thicker than the *Cleistocactus* parent. The small flowers are reminiscent of *Cleistocactus*, but at the tip they open up like small *Echinopsis* flowers.

Coryphantha

When it's not in bloom, this genus of tubercle cacti is indistinguishable from *Mammillaria* cacti. Only a flowering plant displays grooved tubercles that are furrowed at the top, from which the buds and flowers emerge.

This genus includes plants with beautiful, hardy spination, and that develop large flowers. They grow mainly in Mexico and in the southern United States. These cacti need a warm sunny place under glass. They don't do well indoors on a windowsill, but a sunny bay window or a hotbed is fine. They like to be potted in containers larger than would normally be chosen, and they need a clay-rich soil substrate.

It takes these cacti a little longer than others to start their growth period in the spring. Watering should begin later than would otherwise be necessary. These plants flower in the summer and in early autumn. During the winter the soil is kept dry.

Some species develop small offsets that often begin to develop roots while still attached to the mother plant. These offsets are easy to remove and can be cultivated as individual plants, but they won't bloom until they've reached a specific height. They will then develop more wool and fewer spines at the apex, and, typical of this plant, they'll develop grooves in the areoles.

The tubular blossoms of *Cleistocactus tupizensis* have adapted to pollination by hummingbirds.

CLEISTOCACTUS STRAUSII

This plant, covered with snow-white spines and bristles, is readily available. Although its flowers don't develop until the plant is 3 feet (1 m) high, when they do appear, their dark, carmine-red blossoms present a charming contrast to the white spination.

CLEISTOCACTUS TUPIZENSIS

This plant is native to the Tupiza region of Bolivia, so it will tolerate somewhat lower temperatures. This cactus grows straight upwards and has pale reddish-to-fuchsia spination and red, trailing flowers.

CLEISTOCACTUS HYBRIDS

It may seem surprising, considering the wide variety of body shapes and flowers of these groups, but there are indeed hybrids between the genera *Cleisto-*

66

CORYPHANTHA ANDREAE

This species includes cacti with several different shapes. These cacti have bright yellow flowers and rather large, shiny, deep green tubercles that are up to 1" (2.5 cm) wide.

CORYPHANTHA ELEPHANTIDENS

The tubercles on this cactus are up to 2¼" (6 cm) wide and 1½" (4 cm) long. The flowers are conspicuous because their light red to carmine-red color is rare among the *Coryphantha*. These colors create a glorious contrast to the deep green of the body and the white wool at the apex of the plant.

Coryphantha elephantidens. Plainly visible are grooved tubercles on the upper part. Fruit has pushed through the wool in front of the flowers.

Echinocactus

ECHINOCACTUS GRUSONII

In their native habitat, *Echinocacti* grow into barrels up to 3½ feet (1 m) high, and only a mature plant will develop flowers. Young specimens are frequently available. In the Canary Islands one can sometimes find cultivated plants that are 1 foot (30 cm) in diameter, with spectacular spines. In addition to the usual golden yellow spination, many species are also white-spined.

This cactus should not be exposed to temperatures below 50–54 °F (10–12 °C) in the winter and it prefers to stand on a warm surface. Avoid locations where the temperature is low, and where the plant might be exposed to cold drafts. Unsightly "cold spots" might be the result. In the summer the plant loves warmth, but not direct sunshine. Be careful during the first sunny days in spring to avoid burns.

The soil should be porous and the flowerpot should not sit in water. See Care Group 3.

Echinocereus

Cacti lovers are particularly fond of these plants because of their decorative spines, and because their large and spined flowers (usually with green stigmas) last several days. Because they're native to a wide region, the care of each plant depends upon its native habitat. However, all *Echinocereus* plants like hot and sunny locations in the summer. Some of the species grow tall, some thrive only in a greenhouse. Some species, however, can be cultivated in a sunny window or in a hotbed. The soil should be mineral-rich and include well-weathered clay and coarse sand. Begin watering in the spring only when plants show distinct development of flower buds; otherwise the buds will

67

not develop into flowers. Only during its main growth period (in early summer) is the plant watered generously; otherwise water it rather sparingly.

During the winter, soil should remain dry and the plant should be in a well-lit location. If soil is kept dry, some species, like *E. pectinatus, E. reichenbachii, E. triglochidiatus,* and *E. viridiflorus,* are able to withstand temperatures slightly below freezing for a short time. See Care Group 2.

ECHINOCEREUS KNIPPELIANUS

This is a small cactus, usually without spines, and with very flat ribs. Because of its thick tubular root, this plant must not be overwatered. These cacti are often grafted; they thrive well and develop beautiful pink flowers early in spring. The sparsely spined body must be carefully adapted to sunlight, but once used to the sun, it tolerates bright, direct sun well.

Color photo of *Echinocereus pectinatus* can be found on the cover and on page 29.

ECHINOCEREUS PECTINATUS

This species (also representative of a whole group of related cacti) is very attractive with its spined ribs, which vary depending on where they're cultivated, and its often carmine-red flowers that have a bright or greenish white center. The root system of this plant is rather sensitive, and the plant needs a mineral-rich soil and much sun. These cacti do better in a greenhouse or in a hotbed, but a plant that has been grafted on a relatively short host can be placed in a south window or in a bay window with southern exposure.

ECHINOCEREUS PENTALOPHUS

This cactus has only four to six ribs, each about ¾″ (2 cm) wide. The smaller plants of this variety do well on a windowsill (perhaps outside the window on a ledge) or in a hotbed. Lilac-colored flowers develop freely. The plant must be kept dry in the spring, even if the color of the body turns reddish, until flower buds are clearly visible.

ECHINOCEREUS REICHENBACHII AND E. R. VAR. FITCHII

This plant has decorative red-brown-to-snow-white comblike (pectinated) spines depending on the variety, and carmine-red flowers with a darker center. This eager-flowering plant is widely available. Water moderately.

ECHINOCEREUS TRIGLOCHIDIATUS

Grey, square spines are characteristic of this plant. It doesn't bloom easily, but some clones do develop flowers. This cactus is robust and can easily be kept outside from the middle of spring until the middle of autumn on a sunny ledge in front of a window that's protected from driving rain. If the soil is dry, it will tolerate moderate frost rather well. Flowerpots shouldn't be too small and the soil should contain clay. Its flowers are scarlet, and yellowish deeper in the center.

ECHINOCEREUS VIRIDIFLORUS

As the name implies, this variety has greenish yellow flowers that develop in early spring. Spines may be white or brown, and, depending upon where they're grown, the color of the body may vary.

Echinocereus
triglochidiatus

E. viridiflorus

Echinofossulocactus

Cacti of this genus are easy to care for, and because of their typical, lamella-like ribs, they're favorites among cacti lovers. In their native Mexico, these cacti grow on the dry grassland. Consequently, they want a rather humus soil and a bright, but not sun-drenched, location. Since flowers develop early in spring, provide a well-lit winter location. See Care Group 1.

ECHINOFOSSULOCACTUS CRISPATUS

Color photo of *Echinofossulocactus crispatus* appears on page 41.

It's difficult to distinguish among the different varieties of the genus *Echinofossulocactus*. One rather beautiful collection is combined under the name *E. crispatus*. It's interesting to watch the white flowers with the wide, bright-to-dark violet stripe in the middle squeezing through the tangle of thick, long, and sometimes rather flattened spines in the middle.

Echinopsis

The members of this genus distinguish themselves from the larger, related genera *Trichocereus* and *Lobivia* by their flowers, which have a clearly defined circle of stigmas. *Trichocereus* grows into columns, and the tubular flower of the *Lobivia* is usually shorter than that of the *Echinopsis*.

Cacti from the genus *Echinopsis* have been known for some time; their long, white-to-pink-colored, funnel-shaped flowers are not only appreciated by cactus lovers, but they're also favorites of many flower lovers. The genus *Echinopsis* today includes those plants that originally came either from the lowlands of northeastern Argentina, southern Brazil, and Paraguay or those that came from the higher elevations of northwestern Argentina and Bolivia. Depending upon their origin, they have different needs.

ECHINOPSIS ARACHNACANTHA AND E. A. VAR. TORRECILLASENSIS

Spines that lie flat against the plant's body are reminiscent of spiders—the scientific name given to the plant reflects this. This species includes many differently shaped varieties. Even when very young, this plant willingly produces numerous flowers that are mostly yellow or red. A cultivated plant develops new offsets vigorously. See Care Group 4.

ECHINOPSIS AUREA

Spines on this cactus extend normally and the flowers are yellow. This robust plant's spines and flowers develop easily and profusely. General growth varies greatly from plant to plant. See Care Group 4.

ECHINOPSIS EYRIESII

Samples of this genus in its true form are very difficult to find. As early as the 19th century the following plants were imported: *E. eyriesii*, *E. multiplex*, *E. tubiflora*; and very quickly thereafter myriads of hybrids appeared. Some hybrids have long spines, some have short spines, and their flowers are usually white or soft pink. Sometimes some flowers have a dark pink stripe down the middle. The very long, tubular blossoms open at night, and close up again around noon of the following day. This seems to be why some call this plant (wrongly) "Queen of the Night." (This name, however, is correctly reserved for

70

Selenicereus.) The plant produces off-sets that often begin to develop roots while still attached to the mother plant. These offsets are easy to remove. Propagate those plants that are "good" bloomers rather than those that are "lazy" bloomers. The lowland *Echinopsis* likes a rather humus soil mixture and rich, but nitrogen-poor, fertilization, as well as good care. See Care Group 1.

ECHINOPSIS MAMILLOSA VAR. KERMESINA

This plant grows to 6″ (15 cm) in diameter; the body has a fresh green color; flowers are a brilliant carmine-red. The flowers appear a bit flattened, and they don't open all the way. See Care Group 1.

ECHINOPSIS OBREPANDA

A host of different types are sold under this name. These plants come from higher elevations and are robust, but they're rather sensitive to sunburn in early spring. Spines are tough and hooked towards the body. Because of the tuberlike root the plant needs rather porous soil and flowerpots of sufficient depth. Originally its flowers were white, but rose, soft violet, and colors all the way to a deep red are now common. The size of the flower is rather large for the size of the plant. The flower is very beautiful with a slightly turned-up, small outer edge. Don't pamper this plant with improper care. See Care Group 4.

ECHINOPSIS HYBRIDS

The genus *Echinopsis* has much to offer hybrid growers. During the 19th century, a host of *E. eyriesii* hybrids was

produced. After the initial work of German and Czechoslovakian breeders, an American breeder was able, around the time of World War Two, to produce a cross between the large lowland *Echinopsis* (with its long flowers) and the colorful flowers of the highland *Echinopsis* and *Lobivia*. They were listed under the name of "Paramount hybrids," found many friends, and encouraged further crossbreeding. After World War Two a German breeder produced astounding hybrids between *Echinopsis* and *Trichocereus*. In the meantime, further hybrids were produced between *Echinopsis* and *Cleistocactus* and between *Echinopsis* and *Hildewintera*. Today there exists an immense assortment of *Echinopsis* hybrids with differing needs. Different species have different spines and flowers in different sizes, colors, and shapes. Cacti lovers looking for beautiful cacti that are easy to care for and that produce

Echinopsis aurea. The flowers of this plant (compared to other *Echinopsis*) are only medium-long.

71

Espostoa

These cacti, which grow into large columns, like a well-balanced winter climate that's not too cold. They show their full beauty only in a greenhouse environment. Young specimens are often cultivated on the windowsill for their beautiful white covering. These plants cannot be sprayed; lime deposits discolor their white hair. See Care Group 1.

Eulychnia

These cacti also do best in the greenhouse. Young plants with their decorative spines and sometimes furlike, shaggy hair are great favorites, and they're often included in a small cacti collection. See Care Group 1.

Ferocactus

These cacti often grow into large globes. Young plants are very popular because of the powerful, often colored, hooked or ringed spines at the apex that appear particularly large because of the small size of the cactus. Nurseries in the Canary Islands produce decorative plants measuring 12″ (30 cm) in diameter with brilliant spination, particularly the *Ferocactus latispinus*, and the *F. wislizenii*. Both kinds are ideal for a bay window with southern exposure.

Ferocacti love lots of sun and warmth. As was mentioned in the discussion of *Echinocactus grusonii*, temperatures in the winter should not fall below 54 °F (12 °C) and their container should be placed on a warm surface to keep their "feet" warm. See Care Group 2.

One kind of *Echinopsis obrepanda*

Color photo of *Eulychnia saintpieana* appears on page 13.

Echinopsis hybrid "Geisenheim"

flowers willingly are advised to look for an *Echinopsis* hybrid rather than one of the rare specimens. Gardeners who'd like to try to hybridize (if only to observe the process and outcome) will find interesting possibilities among the *Echinopsis* hybrids. See an appropriate Care Group, depending on parent combination: 1, 3, or 4.

Epiphyllum hybrids: See *Phyllocacti*

FEROCACTUS SETISPINUS

These specimens differ from "regular" *Ferocacti* since they're not very large, they have thin spines, and they produce (willingly and continuously) little yellow flowers with a red center. The red fruit is also very decorative. This cactus tolerates cool temperatures in the winter. See Care Group 1.

Gymnocalycium

Most of the *Gymnocalycium* cacti are easily recognized by their rounded ribs located between the areoles and the horizontal grooves. Typical, also, are their flowers, which have large, round, bare scales.

In nature they're distributed over a wide area and, consequently, their needs vary accordingly. But most of them like a rather humus, but porous, soil that should remain slightly acidic. *Gymnocalycium* react unfavorably to basic soil; water used for watering should be free of lime, or used with an appropriate additive.

This green cactus often develops only sparse spination. It likes a well-lit location, but not direct sunlight. From the wide variety available, choose only those cacti that remain small, when space is limited. The varieties mentioned here are all suitable for the windowsill. Most cacti mentioned here fall in Care Group 1.

GYMNOCALYCIUM ANDREAE

This cactus remains small. It's robust, it has a dark green body and it produces brilliant sulphur-yellow flowers that appear without difficulty when the plant is still very young.

Color photo of *Gymnocalycium andreae* appears on page 13.

GYMNOCALYCIUM BALDIANUM

This cactus is similar to the one previously described. It's somewhat larger than *G. andreae*, and it has red to dark red flowers. Probably because of unintentional hybridization, you'll often

Ferocactus setispinus. The picture shows the fruit and (typical for *Ferocacti*) hooked spines at the apex.

Below: *Gymnocalycium baldianum*

73

find mixtures of *G. andreae* and *G. baldianum* (commercially grown) that have orange flowers.

GYMNOCALYCIUM BRUCHII

The density of its spination varies widely. It has pink flowers that develop in early spring.

GYMNOCALYCIUM MIHANOVICHII

The body is brown-green to red-green and has (unusual for *Gymnocalycium*) horizontally striped, sharply defined ribs. This is a slow-growing plant. Since this is a sensitive plant when growing on its own roots, it's often grafted onto another cactus. It doesn't like cold temperatures in the winter. Flowers are white-green. The *G. m.* var. *friedrichii* has pink flowers. See Care Group 1 or 3.

GYMNOCALYCIUM MIHANOVICHII VAR. FRIEDRICHII "RUBRA"

Whenever *G. m.* var. *f. Rubra* cacti are shown in large quantities, it's possible for accidental mutations to occur. Mutations do not have chlorophyll and will, therefore, remain red. Gardeners in Japan recognized a unique possibility and began to graft these seedlings to other bases, because alone they wouldn't survive without chlorophyll. From these experiments we now have cacti with colors that range from brilliant red to yellow to blackberry. All of the plants lack their own chlorophyll, and all must be grafted. Sometimes these cacti even develop flowers. Since there's by nature often a difference in the rate of growth between *G. mihanovichii* and the base cactus, these cacti do not survive very long. Regular care and watering, as well as a well-lit location away from direct sunlight, are all recommended. See Care Group 1 or 3.

GYMNOCALYCIUM MULTIFLORUM

This popular, robust variety produces large, white-to-soft-pink flowers. As its name implies, it flowers in great numbers.

Haageocereus

This column cactus will generally produce flowers only in a greenhouse. However, young plants, because of their beautiful fuchsia-red, yellow, or dark brown spination, are favorites, and they're often added to a cacti collection. The *Haageocereus* wants to be in a sunny, warm location and it needs porous soil. After a short rest period during midsummer, this plant begins another growth phase, during which sufficient watering is important. Temperatures should be kept at about 50–59 °F (10–15 °C) during the winter. See Care Group 3.

Hildewintera

You can't mistake this cactus. Its flowers have an inner circle of small, bright petals. Cacti lovers appreciate their dense, golden yellow spination and the many flowers they produce. *Hildewintera* is an ideal hanging plant, but remember that the branches can grow up to 5 feet (1.5 m) long. See Care Group 1 or 3.

Beautiful and interesting hybrids between *Hildewintera* and *Echinopsis* that grow stocky and upright are available.

Lobivia

The name of this genus is a transposition of the letters of Bolivia, its homeland. The distinct circle of stigmas in the center of the flower is typical of this genus. Compared to *Echinopsis*, its tubelike flowers are shorter and stockier. The ribs are often divided into diagonally arranged knobs. Given the right care, *Lobivia* will thrive and easily produce flowers in great numbers. The flowers don't last more than a day. During hot weather they last only for a few hours. Corresponding to the conditions and elevation of their homeland, they prefer to be kept in a "hardy" environment, and they don't want to be pampered. With insufficient light, spination will be sparse and growth unhealthy. *Lobivia* needs a well-lit and cool location with lots of fresh air; it will suffer if the air is stagnant and hot. Contrast in temperatures between night and day as well as between summer and winter are desirable. The winter rest period must be strictly observed, during which time the plant should be kept dry and cool. Hardy plants will tolerate short periods of night frost, if they're kept dry. General cactus soil is fine, but the soil must be porous for plants with tubular roots. *Lobivia* does poorly in a dark place that always has the same temperature. It thrives in an appropriate hotbed (with its needs kept in mind) or on a windowsill that's not exposed to direct sun, or outdoors on a ledge in front of a window. See Care Group 4.

LOBIVIA DENSISPINA

This is a large cactus, in size, in spination, and in the variety and color of its flowers. The many, comblike spines are conspicuous. Because of its relatively large and colorful flowers, this cactus enjoys great popularity and is easily available, sometimes under the wrong name of *L. famatimensis*. Its tuberlike root system needs porous soil.

LOBIVIA HERTRICHIANA

This cactus is popular because of its large, brilliant red flowers.

LOBIVIA JAJOIANA

The brilliant red or yellow flower, with the deep black center and the circle from which the stigmas rise, is one of the most beautiful cactus flowers. Offsets are seldom produced, but the cactus can be grown from seed.

Color photo of *Lobivia jajoiana* appears on pages 24 and 25.

LOBIVIA SILVESTRII

This plant differs from the rest of its group because of its fingerlike, abundant shoots. Because of this, it was listed

Lobivia densispina with comblike spination close to its body

for a long time as a separate genus, *Chamaecereus*. Shoots can be broken off easily and rooting takes place quickly. This plant is well known and popular because it's easy to root and it produces red flowers abundantly. The plant needs a wide, flat container and humus soil. It should not be pampered, or it will flower poorly and become vulnerable to red spider infestation. It prefers cold and absolutely dry conditions during the winter. The plant will shrink during this time and the shoots might turn reddish. Both conditions are normal.

Hybridization (particularly with other *Lobivia* cacti) has produced a great number of hybrids with a slightly stocky appearance and flowers ranging in color from a rare white to yellow to red and violet-red.

LOBIVIA WRIGHTIANA

Lobivia wrightiana

Characteristic of this plant (when more mature) are its striking, long, soft central spines and the soft pink flowers that develop early in spring.

Color photo of *Mammillaria* can be found on page 25.

Mammillaria

Cacti from this genus enjoy special popularity among cacti lovers. Some gardeners solely cultivate *Mammillaria* and they've been able to put together collections that are worth seeing. *Mammillaria*-lovers have formed their own associations and publish their own journal.

What's striking about *Mammillaria* is the geometrical arrangement of spines, an often delightful contrast to the white woolly covering around the flowering zone. Most of the flowers are small and red, and develop in circles at the apex of the plant. Berries produced after flowering are also very decorative. Characteristic of this genus (and its many varieties) are its smooth tubercles and flowers, which develop deep in the grooves between the axillary tubercles.

Many of the plants in this genus are beautiful, robust, and reliable. Almost all of them, but particularly those that form "cushions," prefer to be in wide, flat containers, and all of them want porous soil to which a good portion of coarse sand has been added. Those that appear white or yellow due to their dense spination or thick hairlike covering love a particularly bright, sunny, and warm location, and they require less watering. Those whose overall appearance is more green prefer a well-lit location that should, however, be protected from direct sunlight. They also like a more humus soil and need more water. Almost all of the cacti mentioned under this heading should be kept dry during the winter, with temperatures of 43–46 °F (6–8 °C). See Care Group 1.

Many *Mammillaria* do well on a windowsill. They'll produce (thanks to the warmth of the springtime sun behind the window glass) decorative flowers in early spring. They're in need of sufficient water then. Oblong *Mammillaria* tend to lean towards the light with the upper part of the body. The gardener will then see more of the less decorative "backside" of the plant. However, don't "balance" by turning the plant.

Although its seeds are relatively small, *Mammillaria* are easy to cultivate from seed, and a plant is often ready to flower within three to four years.

MAMMILLARIA BOCASANA

This plant is interesting due to its dense, white hairlike covering. Its spines (hooked at the end) grow straight out of every areole. Its long red fruits are more conspicuous than its cream-colored flowers.

This plant is sensitive to overwatering; porous soil and sparse watering are recommended.

MAMMILLARIA BOMBYCINA

This cactus is popular and striking because of the contrast between its white wool, its white spines at the edges, and its dark-red-to-brown hooked middle spines.

Flowers are red and develop in the second year, in the spring. To encourage blooming, the plant should be in a well-lit location during the winter. See Care Group 1 or 2.

MAMMILLARIA CAMPTOTRICHA

This plant grows large cushions.

Densely intertwined spines are reminiscent of a bird's nest.

MAMMILLARIA ELEGANS

Under this name (which is disputed by specialists) is a variety of beautiful and popular *Mammillaria* cacti. Its appeal consists of the brightly colored, white spines at the edges, and sometimes darker (almost black) central spines, as well as its red flowers.

MAMMILLARIA ELONGATA

The beauty of this plant lies less in its inconspicuous, yellowish white flowers as in its light-to-dark-yellow spination. It forms groups of decorative, long, fingerlike branches. It prefers a sunny location and a porous soil. Water sparingly.

MAMMILLARIA GRACILIS

These cacti consist of many large individual bodies. Spines are shiny and

Mammillaria elongata. **This type of cactus can easily be propagated from offsets.**

Mammillaria hahn-iana. This type has particularly long and thick hair.

to its characteristic body-hiding, white, hairy covering. Since the extent of the covering varies, choose a plant with dense and long hair. A very bright, sunny location and porous soil is recommended. Water sparsely. Flowers will develop only under favorable conditions. See Care Group 2.

MAMMILLARIA LONGIFLORA

For a *Mammillaria* cactus, this variety has unusually large flowers, approximately 1½″ (4 cm) in diameter. Center spines are hooked. Cacti that develop large flowers are often sensitive, but overall this variety is robust, grows well and develops plenty of flowers if the soil is porous and kept on the dry side. Flowers develop early in spring, which means that during the winter the plant needs a well-lit location.

Mammillaria longiflora

white. Dark spines in the middle at the top do not appear until an advanced age. White flowers appear in the autumn. Individual shoots fall off easily, and they've often developed roots while still on the mother plant. This plant is widely distributed due to ease of propagation.

MAMMILLARIA HAHNIANA

This plant is particularly attractive due

MAMMILLARIA LONGIMAMMA

Characteristic of this plant are its noticeable long tubercles and its bright yellow, relatively large flowers. Tubercles can be cut off cleanly using a sharp knife; allow them to dry sufficiently and they can be cultivated into new plants.

MAMMILLARIA MAGNIMAMMA

Under this name a number of easily differentiated varieties are combined, one of which is particularly popular: *M. centricirrha*. The whole group contains a milky sap and has tubercles. Members of the "green" *Mammillaria* often grow beautiful "cushions" when older, and they're very attractive due to the contrast of the green color of the body, the white of the wool tufts in the axils, and the red of their flowers. This plant needs a well-lit place for the spination to remain strong, but protection from direct midday sun is essential.

MAMMILLARIA MICROHELIA

These column-shaped cacti sometimes develop groups of offsets. Their particularly beautiful spination is reminiscent of a "small sun," as its name implies. This type of cactus has many different variations of spination and blossom color. It's easily available commercially.

MAMMILLARIA PARKINSONII

Because of its brilliant white spination, this plant must be placed in a warm location where full sun is available; reduce watering. A dash of lime fertilizer added to the soil now and then supports healthy spination. Over the years a dicotyl division at the apex of the plant results in the formation of a well-balanced grouping that can reach 20″ (50 cm) in diameter, even when cultivated. The cream-colored flowers are less noticeable; its fruit is red. See Care Group 2.

MAMMILLARIA RHODANTHA

This popular cactus comes in many different varieties. The very even spination is beautiful and can vary in color from yellow to brown. Red flowers develop late in the summer and in the autumn, when most cacti have finished blooming.

MAMMILLARIA THERESAE

This plant was found in the higher regions of Mexico in 1967. Feathered spines and relatively large flowers make it an interesting and beautiful plant. The roots are tuberlike and should, therefore, be placed in porous soil and should not be overwatered. Given that care, the cactus will grow well on its own root system. Grafting this cactus to

another plant is not recommended, since this would deform its already stocky shape.

MAMMILLARIA WOODSII

This collection of cacti with slightly varying shapes had (until quite recently) been included with *M. hahniana*. However, the hair and wool covering this plant are much shorter and sparser,

Mammillaria parkinsonii with red fruit. The "head" in the foreground has developed dichotomously.

Mammillaria theresae

Color photo of *Mammillaria wood-sii* can be found on page 40.

and the spination is much more visible. Flowers are red.

MAMMILLARIA ZEILMANNIANA

This cactus also has hooked center spines, but remains bare between the indentations of the tubercles (in contrast to *M. bocasana*). Young plants willingly produce violet-red (seldom white) flowers. Over the years the plant develops into a group of newly produced shoots. They love to be in wide, flat containers filled with porous soil to which a good amount of coarse sand has been added.

Neoporteria

Many of the cacti of this genus have developed long, tuberlike roots, a dark-to-black body color, or dense spination as a result of the extreme conditions in their native Chile. Although they're difficult to raise in colder northern regions, some of them can be successfully cared for in a small collection, provided one develops a sense of their needs. See Care Group 1.

Neoporteria gerocephala. Flowers won't open any further than can be seen in this photo.

NEOPORTERIA GEROCEPHALA

Spination, dense and intertwined, varies from creamy white to a dark brown. The carmine-red flowers (yellow on the inside) have petals that bend towards each other and do not open, even when the flower has opened up. Flowers bloom in late autumn or early spring. Porous and rather mineral-rich soil is recommended. Water sparingly.

NEOPORTERIA PAUCICOSTATA

This is also a plant of varying shapes. Particularly popular are those with a blue-green body color and black spination. The soft, reddish white flower opens all the way.

Notocactus

Most of the plants from this genus are small ball cacti. They're best recognized by their obvious red-to-purple-colored stigmas. Many varieties of *Notocacti* are well suited for the beginner's small collection. All like somewhat humus-rich soil, as well as a well-lit, warm location. Those that are sparsely spined should not be exposed to direct sunlight. All members of this genus like an even environment, and even in winter they don't like to be too cold or too dry. See Care Group 1.

NOTOCACTUS HASELBERGII

This cactus has an obviously flattened apex. The stigmas are exceptional because of their deep yellow color. This cactus develops flowers (on its slanted top, facing the sun) in early spring.

NOTOCACTUS LENINGHAUSII

This cactus differs from other *Notocacti* by growing into a short column. The golden yellow spination and the yellow flowers that appear when the plant is 8″ (20 cm) high make this a very decorative cactus. The apex grows slanted towards the light. This inclination of the plant towards the sun shouldn't be altered.

NOTOCACTUS OTTONIS

This once was one of the cactus lovers' standard cacti and it's still widely available today. Spination is sparse, and the color of the body green, with a woolly covering at the apex. Location should be well lit but not exposed to direct sunlight. Silky yellow flowers have (true to the species) red stigmas.

NOTOCACTUS SUBMAMMULOSUS VAR. PAMPEANUS

This cactus has bright, unevenly flattened central spines and yellow flowers with a typical red stigma.

Opuntia

Opuntia, with their mostly leaflike, flat branches, are some of the best known cacti. The wild-growing *Opuntia* are common in the Mediterranean area. *Opuntia* need porous soil and full, hot sun, or they will grow thin, unsightly branches. Only very few are suitable for cultivation inside a window. Flowering only takes place with optimal care, and almost all *Opuntia* tend to get very large. However, given the right care, there are those that are beautiful, have blue stripes (sometimes), have decorative spination that will do well, and will flower easily. They do have beautiful spination, but if touched by accident, hundreds of spines with hooks can be-

come lodged in the skin. How to handle such an injury is discussed on page 36. *Opuntia* should, therefore, never be touched with bare hands. See Care Group 1.

OPUNTIA MICRODASYS

This cactus is almost always available commercially. Hair-covered spines make its branches look like little cushions. The color of the hairs covering the brown spines varies from white to yellow to reddish.

Those native to the higher Andean region belong to the subdivision *Tephrocactus* and can be cultivated in a hotbed. See Care Group 4. Some of the winter-hardy *Opuntia* can be planted outdoors, in climates that simulate those of wine-growing regions, with good drainage, or they can be part of a rock garden.

Oreocereus

This species flowers only in the green-

Notocactus haselbergii is one of the first cacti to bloom in the spring.

Color photo of *Opuntia microdasys* can be found on page 12.

81

house. Young plants of these white woolly cacti with powerful spination are also very popular in small cacti collections. However, conditions in its native environment make this cactus less a candidate for cultivation indoors with even temperatures. It can be outside in a hotbed. Lots of fresh air and temperature contrasts between day and night and between summer and winter are all recommended, as is a nightly cool-down after a hot day. The cool-down also increases humidity. See Care Group 4.

OREOCEREUS TROLLII

The body of this cactus is covered with a thick blanket of white wool. Yellow-to-reddish spination is visible through this wool blanket.

Parodia

Oreocereus trollii. In its native habitat, its thick hair protects it against light night frosts.

These cacti are very similar to *Noto-cacti*; however, they don't have red stigmas, but they often have hook-shaped center spines instead. There are many among this genus that are worth

adding to a collection because of their wonderful spination and the abundant flowers they produce. Seeds of this species are very small and sowing them requires some skill. However, once the seedlings have reached the proper height, it's rather easy to cultivate them. See Care Group 1.

PARODIA MUTABILIS

Characteristic of this frequently offered cactus are its strong, yellow spination and its yellow flowers.

PARODIA SCHWEBSIANA

These cacti derive their popularity from their white woolly covering at the apex, which will constantly decorate the plant with newly developing layers over the course of many weeks.

PARODIA SUBTERRANEA
= *P. maassii* var. *subterranea*

This plant is very decorative because of the contrast created by its strong black, hooked spines, the white wool covering surrounding the spines, and its red flowers.

Phyllocacti

Phyllocacti have double-edged, flattened, and (almost always) spineless branches. While most of the cacti in our garden are cultivated from wild cacti, *Phyllocactus* hybrids have been around since the 19th century. Hybridization has produced an ever increasing number of them to this day. The beginning was a cross between the upright-growing, red-flowering *Heliocereus* and *Nopalxochia*. Added to that hybrid was the white-flowering, epiphytic *Epiphyllum crenatum*, and last, but not least, in order to produce even larger flowers, *Selenicereus*, the "Queen of the Night." The shape, size, and varied colors of the flowers have made it one of the most popular indoor plants. Flowers may reach a diameter of 8″ (20 cm) and are among the most beautiful cactus flowers, in brilliant white, yellow, orange, red and violet-red colors.

Different parents produce differences that determine the care they require. Some grow upright, some trail gently, some are small, some are large, some are sensitive, some are less so. Many highly regarded variations come from the United States, where they're selected (under optimal climatic conditions) solely for the beauty of their flowers.

Since epiphytic plants are the basis for these hybrids, they're all potted in ordinary porous potting soil to which sand, perlite, and perhaps sphagnum have been added. They need a well-lit location with partial sun. They bloom better in full sunlight, but the leaves become unsightly when sunburned. During the summer months a place under a tree with partial shade (but protected against midday sun) is ideal. During the winter the plants should be kept around 46–50 °F (8–10 °C) and the soil kept slightly moist. Propagate from broken-off branches. See the section on propagation from cuttings, on page 50. See Care Group 5.

Pilosocereus

PILOSOCEREUS PALMERI

When this plant with its bluish frosting is about 20″ (50 cm) tall, it develops long, decorative wool tufts in its areoles which make it look as if the plant were wearing a wool cap. Only under favor-

able conditions and when it's sufficiently tall do red-brown flowers push through the woolly covering. It's easy to bring this plant into bloom in the greenhouse.

Parodia schwebsiana

P. subterranea

Lobivia or *Mammillaria*. Characteristic are the laterally developing flowers. Almost all other ball cacti develop their flowers at the apex.

Rebutia are popular plants and they're always available. They'll thrive when care instructions are followed. They develop colorful flowers willingly and abundantly in spring. In addition, it's rather easy to grow them from seed. Some bloom the second year. Since they come from rather high elevations, they like well-lit locations but not too much heat. They also need lots of fresh air and pronounced differences in temperature between day and night, as well as between summer and winter. They wither away when exposed to stagnant air and living-room temperatures, and they're also subject to insect infection, particularly by red spider mites. *Rebutia* do excellently in the hotbed, or, during their active growth cycle, outside on a window ledge. Several can be planted together in a low window box in porous soil. During the winter months they should be kept cool and dry; otherwise the development of flowers will be stunted. Individual varieties do vary among each other, and some are often the result of hybridization. See Care Group 4.

Two rather new *Phyllocacti* **hybrids: "Space Rocker" (above), and "Olympic Gold" (below). Color photos of other** *Phyllocacti* **can be found on pages 42 and 45.**

See Care Group 3. Temperatures during the winter months should be about 59 °F (15 °C); keep the soil slightly moist.

Rebutia

Rebutia are small-ribbed, or tuberculated, ball cacti. When not in bloom they can easily be confused with

REBUTIA AUREIFLORA

This is an attractive plant with deep yellow flowers and typically long, hairy bristles ranging from yellow to white.

REBUTIA HELIOSA

The distinctive spination justifies its Latin name, which means "sunlike." The slender, orange-colored flower adds to the beauty of the plant.

Budding creates a group of several offsets. Sometimes in midsummer the plant takes a rest; watering should be reduced then. Propagation from shoots is easy; however, these shoots will usually not develop tubular roots. Grafted plants often appear too massive.

REBUTIA KRAINZIANA

This plant is typical of its genus. It has a dark green body with white dots that look like polka dots at the tip of the areoles, and red flowers. Its place of origin is unknown. This plant should be protected from hot sun. There is one white-blooming variety named "Stirnadel's Masterpiece."

REBUTIA MINUSCULA

This well-known plant is frequently sold in nurseries and specialty stores. Its spination and flowers differ from other *Rebutia*. Spination is rather sparse and protection from direct sun is important.

REBUTIA PERPLEXA

Originally only one plant of this species was found. It's rather easy to grow from seed, which accounts for its wide distribution today. Its lilac-pink flowers make this plant a particularly striking representative of this group of heavily sprouting *Rebutia*. The individual body is rather small.

REBUTIA PYGMAEA

This variety belongs to a group of *Rebutia* that grow cylindrically and create groups of individual shoots by budding. The tuberlike root needs porous soil.

Rebutia aureiflora

Rhipsalidopsis

RHIPSALIDOPSIS GAERTNERI HYBRIDS (EASTER CACTUS)

Like the Christmas cactus, the leaves of

Rebutia krainziana, "Stirnadel's Masterpiece"

5.5) and porous. Use regular potting soil, and add a healthy amount of perlite, peat moss and sphagnum. Soil and water for watering may not contain any lime. The soil should always be moist. This cactus also likes a certain amount of humidity. During the summer months the plant can be placed outside in partial shade. When precipitation is absent, the plant likes a gentle shower from a watering can. A rest period from late autumn to late winter with temperatures around 50 °F (10 °C) and reduced watering support flowering. From late winter on, the plant can be moved to a warmer location. See Care Group 5.

Different shapes of *Rebutia pygmaea*

Easter cactus hybrid *Rhipsalidopsis* × *graeseri* "Quittlinga"

this cactus consist of short, flat sections; however, its flowers are radially symmetrical. It flowers usually near Easter because flowers develop with the lengthening of the days. This epiphytic plant is somewhat sensitive when grown on its own roots. The soil should, therefore, be slightly acidic (pH value of 5 to

Rhipsalis

This plant may have flat branches like the *Phyllocacti*, but some are many-branched and coral-like with thin, round sections. Flowers are very small, and there are often white berries like mistletoe. This epiphytic plant is popular and often used as a companion to orchids, bromeliads, and tillandsia. All have a common native environment, and they all need care that corresponds to that environment. Like the *Rhipsalidopsis*, *Rhipsalis* should have a light soil with plenty of peat moss and an addition of perlite and sphagnum, as well as some parts of substrate meant for orchids (osmunda fibre) and other chopped fern roots. Soil and water for watering should both be slightly acidic.

Most of the branches of most varieties grow downwards in an arch, and are cultivated as hanging plants. A summer location may be in light shade under a tree. The numerous small flowers appear in the winter and the plant should, therefore, be kept in a well-lit and warm place. Glass cabinets for plants or bay

windows for epiphytic plants are ideal. After flowering, numerous berrylike fruits decorate the plant. See Care Group 5.

Schlumbergera

(*Zygocactus*)

SCHLUMBERGERA TRUNCATA HYBRID

Christmas cactus

The Christmas cactus, like the Easter cactus, has branches consisting of many flat, short sections. Aside from the original red-blooming cactus, today's brilliant pink-, white-, and yellow-flowering varieties are just as common. Flowers have adapted to pollination by hummingbirds and (in contrast to the Easter cactus) they're two-sided and symmetrical. In the Northern Hemisphere, flowering occurs around Christmas, during the period of shortening days. Cultivation is similar to that of the *Rhipsalidopsis* and *Rhipsalis* in light, slightly acidic, porous soil. This plant prefers a well-lit location, but not direct sunlight. During the summer it may remain in the same location or be brought outdoors and kept in partial shade under a tree. It should be protected from snails. A short rest period from early to late autumn, with decreased watering but with increased light, helps flowers develop. When flower buds appear, the plant shouldn't be moved or turned, and an even and warm environment should be supplied; otherwise the plant will lose its flower buds. In addition to plants that grow on their own root system, some are grafted to *Pereskia* or *Selenicereus*. See Care Group 5.

Selenicereus

SELENICEREUS GRANDIFLORUS
Queen of the Night

These large cacti have thin, climbing shoots. They belong to a group of particularly popular cacti, even if only a

Closely related to *Rhipsalis* is *Acanthorhipsalis monacantha*.

A new Christmas cactus variety: *Schlumbergera* hybrid "Gold Charm"

Color photo of *Sulcorebutia* can be found on page 37.

few cactus lovers are actually involved in their cultivation. This plant provides an unforgettable experience when several of its large, wonderful flowers open at the same time; some are up to 10″ (25 cm) wide. Flowers open late in the evening and are open only for a few hours; by morning they wilt. The plant is cultivated in a large container in primarily humus, but also porous, soil. Good fertilization is necessary for good growth and the development of bountiful flower buds. The trailing branches should be supported by a sturdy rack. This plant needs a well-lit and warm location, but not direct sunlight. Even in winter the temperature should not go below 59 °F (15 °C). Moderate humidity is also recommended. See Care Group 3.

Setiechinopsis

SETIECHINOPSIS MIRABILIS

This plant constantly produces new batches of its graceful, white flowers that open during the night. Many seeds develop even without outside pollination. See Care Group 1.

Stetsonia

STETSONIA CORYNE

These cacti grow like trees in their native environment. They're often found in cacti seed mixtures. The club-shaped, blue-green young plants with their long, black spination are very decorative. V-shaped grooves develop over the areoles. This plant needs a warm location with minimum temperatures (even in winter) of 59 °F (15 °C). Water moderately. See Care Group 3.

Sulcorebutia

Compared to the shape of *Rebutia's* areoles, those on *Sulcorebutia* are oblong, with comblike spination. Flowers have rather large, wide scales on the outside.

This genus was established in 1951. Before then it was considered a species. In the course of numerous field expeditions, many other beautiful plants were found, and a *Sulcorebutia* fad began to sweep through the ranks of cactus lovers. It's difficult to keep some kind of order among the many catalogue numbers, names, and varieties. Aside from taxonomic problems, *Sulcorebutia* represents a genus comprised of cacti that remain small, have beautiful spination, and have colorful flowers. Since their native habitat is in the higher regions of the Andes, *Sulcorebutia*, like *Lobivia* and *Rebutia*, shouldn't be pampered. They need a well-lit location where temperatures are not too high.

The plant enjoys contrasts in temperature between day and night, as well as between summer and winter. It does not thrive in an even climate inside a heated living room but it does very well in a hotbed, or on a ledge outside a window that's protected from driving rain, with lots of fresh air. Temperatures during the winter should be cool and the soil kept dry. See Care Group 4.

SULCOREBUTIA CANDIAE

This attractive cactus has intertwined yellow spination and brilliant yellow flowers.

SULCOREBUTIA CANIGUERALII

This cactus was named for Father Canigueral, who found it. The red flower

88

with its brilliant yellow center is charming.

SULCOREBUTIA RAUSCHII

This plant is named for the Austrian researcher Walter Rausch. Some of the plants have an almost violet body color, some are brown, and others green. Small spines, lying against the body, and the violet-red flowers create a charming contrast.

SULCOREBUTIA STEINBACHII

These cacti come in a variety of shapes and they sometimes have tough, almost awl-shaped spination in colors that range from yellow to brown and black. The color of the flowers also varies, from yellow to orange to deep violet-red.

Sulcorebutia candiae

Color photo of *Thelocactus bicolor* can be found on page 2.

Thelocactus

This genus includes ribbed as well as tuberculated cacti. Typically for the genus, flowers develop at the end of a short groove. Many cactus lovers are particularly fond of *Thelocactus* because of their tough spination that comes in a variety of colors, and for their large flowers. *Thelocacti* need mineral-rich soil, and during the active growth cycle they need a warm location with full sun exposure. During the winter they can be kept cool and dry. They are ideal for a sunny bay window. See Care Group 2.

THELOCACTUS BICOLOR

Plants of this variety come in different shapes, and *T. bicolor* cacti are widely available. Large, colorful flowers appear in midspring and continue to bloom into autumn.

Trichocereus

These column cacti have a circle of flower petals similar to those of the genera *Echinopsis* and *Lobivia*. Many *Trichocereus* will bloom only in a greenhouse, but young plants with their

Sulcorebutia canigueralii with parti-colored flowers.

Trichocereus hybrid

Trichocereus hybrid "Theleflora"

porous soil, and healthy fertilization. During the summer they prefer a warm location and full sun exposure; during the winter they prefer cool temperatures and dry soil. See Care Group 4.

TRICHOCEREUS FULVILANUS

This plant is popular because of its long, decorative spination. White flowers do not develop until the plant is about 3–5 feet (1–1.5 m) tall.

TRICHOCEREUS HYBRIDS

Hybridization took place between members of the genus *Trichocereus* (like *T. thelegonus*, *T. candicans*, or *T. grandiflorus*) and the genus *Echinopsis*. These hybrids show large, colorful, and beautifully shaped flowers. *Trichocereus* hybrids need a sunny, warm location and soil rich in nutrients. See Care Group 1 or 4, depending upon the parents involved.

beautiful spination are popular additions to small cacti collections.

Even the small variety of this genus will bloom only when given optimal care. *Trichocereus* need a nutritious,

Turbinicarpus

These cacti remain small. With their paperlike, hairy, or feathery spines, they've become increasingly popular.

It's possible to put together a special collection even in a small space; even when still small, these plants will bloom willingly. *Turbinicarpus* cacti survive in their native habitat under very difficult conditions. They grow slowly and should not be sprouted. Mineral-rich, porous soil is recommended because of the tuberlike root.

Several plants are potted together in small but deep containers. Little watering should be done, even during their active growth cycle; too much water might cause the body to burst open along its length. During the summer they need a well-lit and warm location,

90

but not direct sun. In its native habitat the plant is rare, and therefore protected, but it isn't difficult to grow it from seed. See Care Group 1.

TURBINICARPUS VALDEZIANUS

This plant is very popular because of its small, white, feathered spines and its violet-red flowers that develop early in spring. Flower buds are already visible as black dots by the end of winter.

Trichocereus hybrid

Turbinicarpus val-dezianus. Black flower buds are already visible by the end of winter

INDEX

Windows
  bay, 22, 30
  ledges outside, 22–23
  without sunlight, 21
  sunny, 21–22
Winter, care during, 39
Wood lice, 59

Y

Yellow discoloration, 54
Yellow spots, 53

Z

Zygocactus truncatus, see *Schlumbergera truncata* hybrids